D1372515

WITHDRAWN

KNOW YOUR CHILD

Joe Temple

BAKER BOOK HOUSE
Grand Rapids, Michigan

ISBN: 0-8010-8820-8

Printed in the United States of America

To
my beloved Cricket
who "knew our children"

Contents

Foreword

To be asked to write the foreword for a book of this kind is, I consider, a great honor. There will be two divisions of people to whose attention this book may come: (A) those who believe that the Holy Scriptures of the Bible are the inspired, inerrant Word of God—a Book to be studied as a guide to living; and (B) those who do not so believe.

Dr. Temple's book presents no problem to those described in group A, since it is written by one of them and is for them; I consider it an honor to be classed with that group of believers. To those described in group B, I would like to address the following urgent remarks. Very often an immature believer or an unbeliever, or even a skeptic, discerning that a written text is for believers and is in reference to the Bible, will quickly be discouraged in pursuing it because these are things which they do not understand. If you find yourself in such a dilemma let me at this point intercede with your intellectual processes. When in the past you were called upon to study any imperfectly understood subjects in school, you often began the learning of a new truth by being asked to assume certain things to be true; then the author would go on to embellish and amplify his proposition, proving to your human reasoning that the thing which you were originally asked to assume you now could regard as a proven fact.

The point is, if you expect to learn new truth you must enter upon some hitherto unknown territory; and you must be willing to simply assume that some of the author's statements are true until he has had the opportunity to offer the whole story for your consideration. Surely none of us is so erudite as to claim omniscience; therefore, don't go—hear the whole story, especially if you have a child to whom these paragraphs might apply. Then, assuming from Dr. Temple's authoritative presentation and impressive Biblical documentation that he might be right, test it on your own child and let the results speak to you in your own life.

Dr. Temple deals with man's basic emotional endowments and trends as well as with hereditary influences in personality formation and with many personality variations. He discusses husband-wife relationships; maternal overprotection; the results of misplaced desires for approval and power and of psychopathological greed and miserliness. He offers suggestions for attaining maturity; he speaks of human individuality and of rebellious and intransigent conduct. In general, this series covers all of the commonly-met-with characteristics and immaturities —all spoken of in Biblical terms, with their Scriptural descriptions carefully documented. The meticulousness with which the author has searched out and exegeted the original Greek and Hebrew of significant Biblical terms attests to his analytical thoroughness, resulting from his own wide personal experiences and devotion to his task. Throughout the entire text shines the author's confident faith in God, in Jesus Christ, and in the power of the Holy Spirit in all human life.

Frequently, personal illustrations paint for us a picture of Dr. Temple's homelife, where he and his loving wife (now deceased) and their seven children have amply illustrated the workability of the system of child knowledge and training contained in this text. It is certainly fitting that any dissertation on child training should bring up examples of parents—their character and their duties and obligations. Dr. Temple's excursions into marital attitudes and the fundamental principles of marital "chain-of-command" administration are drawn from his wide experience and from Biblical references. Based on observations in my psychiatric practice when working with those involved in insecure marriages, I am convinced that these rules for living and for operating a marriage will undoubtedly prove the most successful counseling one could get.

Dr. Temple is a "specialist," a specialist in a discipline that is built upon the unchangeable wisdom of God—the only thing that is basic and unvariable in our life experience. Because Joe Temple is a "specialist" called by God, it is fitting that he should talk of the training of children and the conduct of their parents in the terminology of God's Book which, for Joe Temple and the rest of us who are believers, contains the basic "rules for life." It is also to be noted, in keeping with our knowledge of the One who inspired the Bible, that when He gives wisdom to one of His servants, as He has to Dr. Temple, it is extremely practical in its application to the "here and now"—it it *relevant* wisdom. It is, therefore, not surprising that the suggestions for knowing and guiding your child, and for the conduct and family life of parents, are practical and relevant to the present age—they *work*. With these thoughts, I commend this book to your close attention and study.

John C. Montgomery, M.D.
Dallas, Texas

Preface

This book is the compilation of a series of lectures which I presented to a class of young parents, and which were taped and transcribed.

By the grace of God, my wife and I have had a measure of success in training our seven children. Realizing that many modern principles of child training are inconsistent with our Christian testimony, we searched the Scriptures that we might know "how to order the child, and how we should do unto him" (Judg. 13:12). The lectures comprised much of what we had gleaned from the Scriptures and put into practice with our own children.

As parents we have been asked many questions. As a pastor, my counsel has been sought. I offer the lectures not as if they present the final word, but rather to share them with the prayer that they may be helpful to others.

Some four thousand sets of the lectures have been distributed in multilith form. It was felt by many that such a reception warranted their publication in a bound book. My son, Tim Temple, pastor of Grace Church in Wichita Falls, Texas, has reduced the lectures for such publication. I am indebted to him for the many hours spent in this endeavor. I am also indebted to the volunteers of our Printed Page Ministry who have shared in typing and other preparation.

There are two observations I would like to make. First, many of the things I have said will be contradicted by certain works on pedagogy and child psychology. This is to be expected, since my studies are based solely on the Scriptures. "The natural man receiveth not the things of the Spirit of God . . . neither can he know them" (I Cor. 2:14).

Second, it is impossible to deal with a subject of this nature without touching upon theological questions concerning which there is disagreement even among sincere Christians. I have dealt with these questions in Christian charity, and I trust my comments will be received in the same spirit.

Joe Temple
Abilene, Texas

1

The Bow Is Bent

Some of the basic questions asked in relation to child training are: "When and how do I begin to train my child?" "How do I train my child at a particular age?" and "Should I try various methods and procedures as I go along?"

The time when you begin really to train your child and the manner in which you train your child depend on how well you *know* your child. If there is one basic thing that parents must realize about training children, it is that they must know their children.

There is a modern suggestion that parents should be "buddy-buddy" with their children: that fathers should be pals with their sons and that mothers should be chummy with their daughters. One who has read very much on the subject or who has had opportunity to talk with some of the children will know, however, that there are many boys who wish that their father would be a father to them, and many girls who wish that their mother would act her age and be a mother to them and not a chum. So when we use the phrase "knowing your child," we do not have reference to the amount of time you spend with your child, playing ball or doing this or that. Rather, we have in mind the idea of making a very definite study of your child, and from this standpoint, "knowing" your child.

Proverbs 22 gives the vital Scriptural foundation for this type of training. One who may have all the experience in the world in training children, but who misses this point, will have a very difficult time in making his other training effective over a long period of time.

Verse 6 is familiar. Many sermons have been preached on it and many parents have claimed it as a promise for the training of their children:

6 Train up a child in the way he should go: and when he is old, he will not depart from it.

One of the commonly accepted interpretations of this passage is that it means to be sure your child is in church and Sunday school every Sunday and be sure he learns a few verses of Scripture. Then after he sows his wild oats, when he is old and gray-headed and too decrepit to do anything else, he will come back to the Lord. You can be sure of that.

This interpretation does not lend much comfort. People who in their later years decline to do what they are actually incapable of doing to begin with, are not very impressive. If that is all the verse means, then it is not very much of a promise.

Another commonly accepted interpretation of the verse is that if you train up a child in the way he should go, when he is old (in this instance the phrase "when he is old" is interpreted to mean "when he is mature")—when he is old enough to make decisions for himself—then he will not depart from the training he has had. This interpretation is basically correct, because in the original text the phrase "when he is old" literally means "when he is mature and at the point where he is able to make decisions for himself." Of course that age varies with different children, and on the basis of different localities and different backgrounds.

But even those who teach this interpretation say, "Be sure that your children go to church and Sunday school, and be sure you teach them to read the Bible." Those who know perhaps a little more of spiritual things say, "Be sure that they have had a personal experience of grace in their hearts, that you have led them to the Lord, that they have accepted Christ as their Savior; then, when they have grown to maturity, they will not depart from the training you have given them."

But if that is what this verse of Scripture means, evidently it is not true in every case. Each of us can probably make reference to our own families or to other people whom we know whose children have been "reared in the church," as we say, and have had every good opportunity in life, but have just gone wild. They have just "gone to the devil," so to speak. They give no evidence at all that they were ever trained correctly.

The usual reaction to such a situation is to think that the parents of such a child were too strict; they should not have made him go to church so much. This type of reaction is usual for any promise in the Word of God that apparently has not proven to be true in a particular situation.

The reason we have mentioned these various interpretations is that all of them are incorrect, either in part or entirely. Look at the verse again, and we will try to ascertain what it does mean because it is so important to understand it in relation to knowing your child.

The Amplified Version of the Old Testament translates the verse in this way: "Train up a child in the way he should go [and in keeping with his individual gifts or bent], and when he is old he will not depart from it." The part of the verse of particular interest to us at this point is that which says "in keeping with his individual gifts or bent." This verse emphasizes the individuality of the child, and that is of extreme importance.

If a parent is to know his child, he will have to realize first of all that his child is an individual. No set rule or group of rules will work for every child. What has worked with my children will not necessarily be successful in the training of your children. And, perhaps of even greater importance, what has worked for one of my children will not necessarily work for all of my children because each child is an individual.

One of the greatest efforts a parent should put forth is the effort to know exactly what his child is like, because a blanket statement such as "just train up a child in the way he should go, and when he is old he will not depart from it" will not work. There are ample illustrations of the truth of this fact in the Bible.

Consider, for example, the family of Adam and Eve. Two children were born into that family. One was Cain, and one was Abel. They had the same type of training, religiously speaking, yet one of them became what today we would term a liberal, and the other became a real student of the Word of God. One of them turned out to be a murderer and the other was murdered. Yet they were reared in the same family and in the same environment.

Another Biblical example is that of Jacob and Esau. They were

4 / Know Your Child

reared in the same family and in the same environment, but one of them became so spiritually inclined that God referred to him as a prince, and the other so inclined toward things of the flesh that God referred to him as a "profane" man. But they were reared in the same home and in all probability had the same training.

Again, consider two of David's children. One of them was Absalom, a murderer, and the other was Solomon, the wisest man who ever lived. Generally speaking, they had the same training in their home, but they definitely did not turn out the same way.

So it should be emphasized, even at the risk of repetition, that it is very important to recognize the individuality of your child.

Look at the verse again and notice the word "way." It is a translation of a Hebrew word that pictures a bow that is bent to launch an arrow in a certain direction. In Psalm 11:1-2, as a matter of fact, you will find the word translated exactly in that way:

> 1 In the Lord put I my trust: how say ye to my soul, Flee as a bird to your mountain?
> 2 For, lo, the wicked bend their bow, they make ready their arrow upon the string, that they may privily shoot at the upright in heart.

Notice the phrase, "the wicked bend their bow." In your Bible the word "their" is in italics. That means it is not in the original text. So the two words "bend" and "bow" go together. These two words are translations of the one Hebrew word which is translated "way" in Proverbs 22:6.

This simply means that when you train a child you need to recognize the direction in which the bow is bent. If you try to bend it in the opposite direction, the bow will break. But if you bend it in the direction in which it is already started, you are training the child properly. Another way of stating it might be to say that if you take into consideration the way in which the bow is bent, and loose the string on the bow, so to speak, before you try to straighten the bow out, you will be training the child in the way he should go.

This word "way" has that picture of the bow back of it, but it has been translated in various ways. It has been translated as "a course of life." It has been translated as "a well-traveled road." It has been translated as "a course of action which is plainly set."

These suggestions indicate that we do not have a pliable piece of clay with which to work when we train our children, as some would suggest. Rather, we have a child whose "bent" is already established. If you want to train your child blindly, just try any old thing on him that you want to try and hope for the best. But if you want to train your child successfully, make a study of your child. Find out in which direction the bow is bent and arrange your training accordingly.

Proverbs 22:6 has another phrase that underscores this truth. Notice the phrase "should go." We would ordinarily think that that phrase contains a translation of the Hebrew word for "go." But this is not the case at all. The phrase "should go" is the translation of a Hebrew word that involves the idea of "appointment," or "a predetermined action."

In the Second Book of Samuel is an illustration of the translation of this word with just that thought. Keep in mind that we are not interested at this point in an exegesis of this verse. We are looking at it only to see how this particular phrase is used so that we will be able to see the meaning of the Hebrew word that is translated "should go." In II Samuel 13:30-32 we read:

> 30 It came to pass, while they were in the way, that tidings came to David, saying, Absalom hath slain all of the king's sons, and there is not one of them left.
> 31 Then the king arose, and tare his garments, and lay on the earth; and all his servants stood by with their clothes rent.
> 32 And Jonadab, the son of Shimeah David's brother, answered and said, Let not my lord suppose that they have slain all the young men the king's sons; for Amnon only is dead: for by the appointment of Absalom this hath been determined from the day that he forced his sister Tamar.

In the background of this story, Amnon had committed an act of incest with his sister Tamar, who was the blood sister of Absalom. Absalom never forgave Amnon for it. He finally arranged a gathering where Amnon would be ambushed and killed. David, when he heard about it, was very upset. But Jonadab said, "Don't feel as bad as you look, because not all your sons are dead; only Amnon is dead." Then he went on to say that Amnon was dead by the "appointment" of Absalom. The word "appointment" is a translation of the Hebrew word that is translated "should go" in Proverbs 22:6.

A very literal translation, without thought of euphony or diction, but just to get the meaning of these two words in this verse, might render Proverbs 22:6:

> Train up a child in the way he should go, with an understanding of how the bow has been bent by appointment or certain predetermined things.

Think of your child not as a piece of pliable clay that can be molded any way you want to mold it; rather, think of him as a bow already bent in a certain way. You have to deal in this fashion with this child who has been placed in your hands.

Many of the people who are suffering mental stress and who have emotional problems in our day are people whose parents trained them according to the parents' bent. There are men today in various professions who are failures, or who are under great stress and strain, because their parents have chosen their profession for them and forced them into it. Therefore, they have no taste for it and do not enjoy it. Parents must realize that it is important to train children according to their individual bent.

There is one other word in this verse that should be noticed, and that is the word "train." It will bear out everything we have suggested thus far. The word "train" is a translation of a Hebrew word that involves several ideas. It involves the idea of dedication, for example. It is so translated in I Kings 8:63. But some of the ideas suggested by this word are from its use in everyday Hebrew—that is, not in the Bible. We might refer to this as "classical Hebrew." In that sense, this word conveys the idea of "initiation" or "introduction." The reason we are making reference to this type of language is that there is no illustration of this particular usage in the Bible. But the word in everyday usage involves this idea, and it is important to the subject of child training.

On the basis of this, then, if you are to train your child properly, there are some things into which you will initiate him because it is your responsibility. There will be some things with which he is not familiar to which you will introduce him.

The word "train" also conveys the idea of throttling something that is about to get out of hand. It even carries the basic idea of choking someone. Now, you might reach the place where you feel like choking your children occasionally, but this is not to suggest that you go that far. To understand fully the meaning of this word "train," however, you must realize that as a Christian parent you will need to throttle certain tendencies that you see in your child.

For example, when your child loses his temper, instead of sitting by and letting him bang his head on the floor until he gets it out of his system, you should throttle that tendency. Of course this is diametrically opposed to what you will find in most child psychology books, but this is what the Word of God affirms. Throttle the tendency; don't let the child always have his way.

This verse of Scripture, then, is not one which suggests that parents should believe in and practice the "behaviorism theory" of child training. You have the responsibility. Train up a child according to the direction in which he is bent, and when he is old enough to make his own decisions, he will not depart from the training you have given him.

Thus far we have stressed understanding the individuality of your child. But how can you accomplish this? In this regard, there is one thing you must keep in mind, and that is that your child is born with tendencies to both good and evil. He does not develop those tendencies after he is born; he is born with the tendencies.

The tendencies toward good are a study within themselves and will be more fully discussed later, but the tendencies toward evil that you will find in your child bear some discussion at this point.

To begin with, we must realize that the tendencies toward evil must be dealt with from both a general and a specific standpoint. My children were born with some general tendencies toward evil, just as your children were. But my children were born with some specific tendencies toward evil with which your children may not have been born, because their ancestors are not the same.

The general tendencies can be dealt with first by taking a look at Psalm 51:5. This is a prayer which David prayed at a time when he was very conscious of the sin in his life:

> Behold, I was shapen in iniquity; and in sin did my mother conceive me.

Some interpret this to mean that the sex act that brings children into the world is inherently sinful. That is not at all what David had in mind. The Amplified Version of the Old Testament makes that clear. It reads:

Behold, I was brought forth in [a state of] iniquity; my mother was sinful who conceived me [and I too am sinful].

This verse says, then, that every child who is born into this world is sinful. He is born in iniquity. He is born, as the theologians say, "totally depraved." He is born not with a tendency to do good, but with a tendency to do evil; not with a desire to do what is right, but with a desire to do what is wrong. Psalm 58:3 confirms this:

The wicked are estranged from the womb: they go astray as soon as they are born, speaking lies.

The Amplified Version's treatment of that verse is:

The ungodly are perverse and estranged from the womb; they go astray as soon as they are born, speaking lies.

Both translations of this verse emphasize that children are perverse. Why is it so important for us to recognize that fact?

Sometimes a father or mother will say in sheer exasperation, "I cannot imagine how I gave birth to somebody like you. You are not like us at all." If such parents would recognize that the child's being their son has no connection with his perversity, they would not make such a statement. That child is born into the world, as is every other child, with a tendency to do evil. If you can get this straight in your thinking, you won't be saying such things as "I can't understand why you want to lie; I don't tell lies." The reason your child tells lies is that he was born a liar. If you don't recognize and accept that fact, you will not be able to train your child effectively.

If you are wondering why we are so insistent on this, turn to Genesis 5:1 and notice what is recorded about Adam, our first ancestor (and remember, we are all related to him):

This is the book of the generations of Adam. In the day that God created man, in the likeness of God made he him.

When you hold your baby in your arms for the first time, it is such a tremendous experience that you cannot possibly feel that this child was created in any other image than the image of God. There is just nothing else so sweet and innocent as a newborn baby. It is hard for anybody to believe that those little babies are born liars. If there were nothing after verse 1 of this passage, that would not be the case, for the verse says that Adam was created in the image of God, and God does not lie. But notice the words of verse 2:

> Male and female created he them; and blessed them, and called their name Adam, in the day when they were created.

Verse 3 begins with the words:

> And Adam lived an hundred and thirty years. . . .

In between the last statement of verse 2 and the first statement of verse 3, Adam sinned and fell short of the glory of God. The next statement of verse 3 is:

> . . . and begat a son in his own likeness. . . .

Notice that! Not in the image of God, but "in his own likeness." So every child born into the world from that day until this is born with what is commonly referred to as "the Adamic nature." As long as the Adamic nature is present in a child, you will have to deal with it in your training. If you forget that it is there, you will never be successful in training your children.

Proverbs 29:15 says:

> The rod and reproof give wisdom: but a child left to himself bringeth his mother to shame.

At the moment we are not interested in the first part of that verse, "The rod and reproof." We will touch on that when we deal with methods of training children. We are interested, however, in the last part of the verse: "a child left to himself bringeth his mother to shame." If you want a child to be a shame to his parents, just let him grow up in the original condition in which he was born. That is the literal meaning of this verse. A better translation of the phrase might be, "A child left in the original condition in which he was born bringeth his mother to shame." On the basis of this, then, we can say that if you let a child go on with his Adamic nature, without any type of training at all, without any rod and reproof, he will bring his parents to shame.

From a moral standpoint, a child left in the original condition in which he was born will not do what is right; he will do what is wrong. That will be his natural tendency. Children have to be taught not to do wrong.

Sometimes the question is asked, "Do you think it is wise to teach your children the Ten Commandments in this Age of

Grace?'' Absolutely! You had better teach them the Ten Commandments even if they never receive the Lord Jesus Christ as their personal Savior. A man who does not lie is better off than one who does, whether he is a Christian or not. You had better teach him, "Thou shalt not kill," because his tendency will be to kill.

A great deal that is blamed on television and movies today —though they do have their serious faults—should be blamed on Adam, and on the fact that our children are "doing what comes naturally" unless we parents do something to interrupt.

In knowing and understanding your child, you must recognize that he is the son of Adam, even though he bears your name. He has all the tendencies that sin can put into a human heart. He was born that way. Unless something is done to change his course, he will continue that way.

"Train up a child in the way the bow is bent. . . ." At this stage in our discussion, the bow is bent toward evil. We are not suggesting that you encourage his evil tendencies; we are suggesting that you train up your child with the understanding that the bow is bent that way. Keep that in mind, and you will find that many of the things that your children do that you cannot understand can be traced back to that fact.

One last thing to be remembered is this: Do not interfere with the natural bent unless you do it intelligently. Some fathers have said to their children, "You are not going to lie; if you do, I'll beat you half to death," and the children go right on lying. That father has interfered without considering the natural bent. Some fathers have said to their daughters, "You girls are going to be pure and good, and if I ever hear otherwise, I'll kill you," and the daughters go right on being impure. Why is this true? Because parents who use such techniques are interfering without understanding the natural bent of the individual child.

2

Problems that Great-Great-Grandfather Started

In Exodus 34:7 there is a very interesting statement that is often misunderstood; it is speaking of God:

> Keeping mercy for thousands, forgiving iniquity and transgression and sin, and that will by no means clear the guilty; visiting the iniquity of the fathers upon the children, and upon the children's children, unto the third and to the fourth generation.

When they read this verse for the first time, many people are disturbed, because it seems to indicate vengeance on the part of God. It seems that God is saying in so many words, "If you disobey Me I will take it out on your children and your grandchildren." That does not seem consistent with our understanding of the nature of God. As we begin to search out what the Word of God has to say, however, we discover that this verse, instead of portraying the vengeance of God, actually portrays the mercy of God. In other words, the beginning of the verse could be read in this way:

> Keeping mercy for thousands, forgiving iniquity and transgression and sin, and they will not be utterly destroyed.

You will notice in the King James Version of the Bible that the word "guilty" is in italics. That, as you may know, is the translators' way of letting you know that it is not in the original text. God is not saying here that He will not clear the guilty. Although other passages teach that, it is not the point of this particular statement.

What He is saying here is that He will not utterly destroy; He will visit the iniquity of the fathers unto the third and fourth generation, and He will stop it there.

What God is saying, then, is not that He is going to get even with us for disobeying Him by making it difficult for our children and grandchildren; rather, God is going to interrupt a natural course of events which we have started, and He will stop it at the third and fourth generations. If He did not, the entire human race would eventually be blotted out. We will not take the time to discuss this from a physical standpoint. If you are interested in pursuing it, there are available to families a number of books about sicknesses and diseases in children. You can read in any such medical book a discussion of how we inherit certain physical weaknesses from our grandfathers and our great-grandfathers. Certain diseases and tendencies to diseases are handed down from grandfather to father to child; there can be no question about that. We are even learning today, because this is a field in which new discoveries are being made continually, that in many cases emotional disturbances in our children can be traced back two or three generations.

The Word of God declared this a long time ago, but it is only now being verified by facts. We will not discuss physical and emotional problems as related to this verse, because much has been written on the subject. But we would like at this point to discuss the spiritual and moral problems that we have with our children because of what their grandfathers and great-grandfathers were.

Much could be said on both sides of the issue of heredity or environment and their respective roles in the development of children. We could discuss this in some detail and still not come to any definite conclusion, because it has never been conclusively settled. It is difficult to determine where heredity ends and environment begins. It can be agreed, however, that regardless of how much in connection with moral problems may be inherited through the blood stream, the atmosphere in which children and grandchildren are reared will show this verse of Scripture to be true.

There is an interesting illustration in the Word of God that verifies the verse of Scripture about which we are thinking. Genesis 20 contains the story of Abraham. It describes an experience that started a ball rolling that got completely out of hand by the time it reached the third generation. It is the story of a man who lied. Because he was afraid that the men of various countries through which he traveled would kill him and steal his beautiful wife, he told everyone that she was his sister. In a sense he was the worst kind of liar. A man who lies outright is bad enough, but a man who lies by telling half-truths is even worse. Abraham justified his lying by the fact that she was his half sister. They did have one parent in common. But he certainly did not treat her like a sister; they lived together as man and wife.

Abraham was a liar, and he accomplished his feat by telling half-truths. There is another factor that is difficult here, exceedingly so: Abraham was a religious liar. That presents a real problem. You may not be surprised when some known crook lies to you; you might almost expect it. But when a prophet of God lies to you, you do not know what to think, because you cannot depend on anything he says from that point on. Whether we like to think it or not, men of God do tell lies. Abraham did; he told a lie, using a half-truth to do it.

If you will turn to Genesis 26:6-11, you will notice a repetition of this very type of incident. This time, however, it was not a repetition in the life of Abraham; it occurred in the life of Abraham's son. What the father had done, the son also was willing to do:

> 6 And Isaac dwelt in Gerar:
> 7 And the men of the place asked him of his wife; and he said, She is my sister: for he feared to say, She is my wife; lest, said he, the men of the place should kill me for Rebekah; because she was fair to look upon.
> 8 And it came to pass, when he had been there a long time, that Abimelech king of the Philistines looked out at a window, and saw, and behold, Isaac was sporting with Rebekah his wife.
> 9 And Abimelech called Isaac, and said, Behold, of a surety she is thy wife: and how saidst thou, She is my sister? And Isaac said unto him, Because I said, Lest I die for her.
> 10 And Abimelech said, What is this thou hast done unto us? one of the people might lightly have lien with thy wife, and thou shouldest have brought guiltiness upon us.
> 11 And Abimelech charged all his people, saying, He that toucheth this man or his wife shall surely be put to death.

One generation later, the son was committing the same sin that the father had committed. The tendency to lie ran in the family. It was an inherited tendency.

The thing that makes this particular family history valuable for our purposes is that it is possible to go down to the third generation of the family and see what effect the lying of grandfather Abraham had on that generation. If you will turn to Genesis 25, you will find the story of Abraham's grandson, Jacob. Jacob turned out to be a persistent liar. His entire life was marked by deceit and lying. From the time he was born until he was an old, old man he lied, when it would have been easier to tell the truth.

If you are familiar with the story of Jacob, you will remember several instances when he lied. We will look at the details of one or two of those instances a little further along because of the individual lessons they have to teach us. But before we do, it would be good to look at Genesis 43, to see verification of the fact that he lied all his life long. In this chapter is found the story of Jacob's sons returning from Egypt and reporting to their father. They reported that their brother Joseph, though they did not know then that he was their brother, would not let them come back into Egypt unless they should bring their younger brother, Benjamin, with them.

What did Jacob say to his sons? Did he say, "Well, boys, there is nothing we can do; let us send Benjamin and trust God"? No, he did not. Notice verse 6:

> And Israel [the Biblical name for Jacob] said, Wherefore dealt ye so ill with me, as to tell the man whether ye had yet a brother?

You will remember that Joseph had asked, "How many of you are there?" and they told the truth. They said, "We are all here except two. One of them is dead [because they thought Joseph was dead] and the other one is back home with Dad." Jacob said, "Why in the world did you tell him that? Why did you not say that all of you were right there in front of him?"

Here he is an old, old man, and at the end of his life he is still lying. However, in line with the subject under discussion, we must realize that it was not entirely Jacob's fault. It was also Abraham's fault. And it was Isaac's and Rebekah's fault. They should have known that this tendency lay within the family, and they should have done something about it. If they had done something about it, they possibly could have made a truthful man instead of a liar out of Jacob.

Perhaps you are wondering at this point how they could have known it. Proverbs 20:11-12 is taught to children a great many times in children's Bible classes. Although these verses undoubtedly do the child some good, they were not intended primarily for children. These verses were written for the instruction of parents:

11 Even a child is known by his doings, whether his work be pure, and whether it be right.
12 The hearing ear, and the seeing eye, the Lord hath made even both of them.

These two verses should be read together, connecting the truth of them, which is this: God has given you as parents eyes that can see. He has given you ears that can hear. A child is known by his doings. Watch what he is doing. Listen to what he says. That is the way you will know and understand your child. If you hear him tell a lie, do not smile and say, "Well, the precious little thing does not know what he is saying." Recognize, rather, that the first lie he tells is an indication that he is a son of Adam, and *you* will have to deal with it.

Recognize secondly that he could have inherited the tendency to lie from his great-grandfather, and even from his father and mother. When you observe that, then take steps to do something about it. Recognize that some children have this tendency to lie, whereas other children do not have it. Within the same family some children may have a tendency to lie and others will not. In thinking about the problems that great-great-grandfather started, we must remember that not every child in your family will have exactly the same problems. If you are not able to recognize the difference in the problems, your task will be exceedingly difficult.

Jacob and Esau are a case in point. Notice what is said about these two brothers in Genesis 25:21-26:

21 And Isaac intreated the Lord for his wife, because she was barren: and the Lord was intreated of him, and Rebekah his wife conceived.
22 And the children struggled together within her; and she said, If it be so, why am I thus? And she went to enquire of the Lord.
23 And the Lord said unto her, Two nations are in thy womb,

and two manner of people shall be separated from thy bowels; and the one people shall be stronger than the other people; and the elder shall serve the younger.

24 And when her days to be delivered were fulfilled, behold, there were twins in her womb.

25 And the first came out red, all over like an hairy garment; and they called his name Esau.

26 And after that came his brother out, and his hand took hold on Esau's heel; and his name was called Jacob: and Isaac was threescore years old when she bare them.

The second twin that was born was called Jacob, and Jacob means "deceiver" or "supplanter." We are told that there was a struggle going on in the womb of the mother of these boys, and it seems that Jacob had the very nature of deceit in him; he endeavored to supplant his older brother as the firstborn of his father by catching him by the heel even in the process of birth.

This passage of Scripture reaffirms that some children are born with the bow already bent, and we need to find out the direction in which the bow is bent so that we can do something about it.

Notice the difference in the personalities of these boys, because it created a problem in the home. This is as modern as if we were to hear it presented in a conference room in consultation with parents today. Genesis 25:27 reads:

And the boys grew: and Esau was a cunning hunter, a man of the field; and Jacob was a plain man, dwelling in tents.

Esau was a cunning hunter. He was an outdoor man, and Jacob was a plain man. The word "plain" here involves the idea of his being effeminate as well. Jacob was what today we would call a little sissy. Esau was a man who loved all sorts of outdoor activities, and Jacob was a little sissy who wanted to stay at home and be a mamma's boy.

How could there be a greater contrast between two children than that? Yet they had the same father, the same mother, and the same home. If Isaac and Rebekah had made any effort to know their children, they could have avoided a great many conflicts. These boys were not studied and directed according to their individual bents. Instead, they so influenced their father and mother that they caused a division in the family. Isaac was an outdoor man himself, and he loved things related to the out-of-doors. Automatically he was drawn to Esau. That is what is said in verse 28:

> And Isaac loved Esau, because he did eat of his venison. . . .

He didn't have much use for Jacob. He was like some fathers you hear about today who look upon their child who may be a weakling, and say, "I don't see how I ever spawned anything like that." They have no real interest in the child and are halfway ashamed of him, berating and riding him almost to the point of desperation because the child does not measure up to what the father had hoped to see in him. That was exactly Isaac's attitude toward Jacob, and Rebekah had the same attitude toward Esau.

This is the third generation. What do we find as we read on in these chapters? There came a time when Esau was to receive the parental blessing, which would amount today to his becoming the official heir, inheriting all the rights of his father. He was to be the executor of the estate, so to speak. There was a special procedure whereby this was to be done. The father had to lay his hands upon the son and pronounce the parental blessing. By this time Isaac was old and blind. He said to Esau, "Son, I would like for us to have one more hunting trip before I die. You go out and get some venison and bring it around, and make a mess of pottage, and we will have one last good time."

Rebekah heard their conversation, and immediately she thought, "That wild little rascal, he is not going to get what Jacob ought to have." What did she do? She called Jacob in and said, "Son, I just heard your father talking to Esau, and Esau is about to get all of the things that you ought to have. Something has to be done!" Well, spineless Jacob, weak as he could be, said, "But, Mom, what can we do? There is nothing we can do. Dad likes Esau, and he is going to give everything to him." She said, "You just leave it all to Mother; she'll take care of it."

And sure enough, she did. She had Jacob go out and kill two kids. Remember, all of this was her idea. She put a skin on Jacob, and then she made a mess of pottage for him. Then she had Jacob take it in to Isaac. Poor old Isaac, who passed on the trait of lying to his family, was deceived by his own son.

The tragic thing about this is that the mother aided and abetted the whole thing. It is an absolute essential for parents to stand together in the training of their children. Many of the problems between Jacob and Esau developed because their father and their mother did not stand together in their training. Rebekah was partial to Jacob and Isaac was partial to Esau. As it turned out, Jacob found himself in serious circumstances because of what his mother did.

It is interesting to notice Rebekah's conniving in this situation. Genesis states the case very clearly. Keep in mind that Esau had it in for Jacob. He said in effect, "That little liar beat me out of my inheritance; I'll fix him!" Rebekah knew what was about to happen, so she did a little conniving. Genesis 27:46 reads:

> And Rebekah said to Isaac, I am weary of my life because of the daughters of Heth: if Jacob take a wife of the daughters of Heth, such as these which are of the daughters of the land, what good shall my life do me?

Why did she say that? Esau had married one of the daughters of Heth, and Rebekah said, "If I get another daughter-in-law in Jacob's wife such as I already have in Esau's wife, I won't be able to live. My nerves are shot, they are frayed, I cannot stand another thing. I have taken about all I can take, and if Jacob marries a girl like the one Esau married, it will just be too much." Meek old Isaac said, "Well, what do you think we ought to do?" "I think Jacob ought to go back to our home country and get himself a wife. I do not think he should stay around here," came the reply. Actually, she was not too much interested in Jacob's getting a wife. She was interested in Jacob's getting out of the country, and this was the only way she could get Isaac to pay the bill. You see, that is just how deceitful and conniving she was.

Well, Jacob got out of the country; but think about Esau for a moment. He seems to have gotten a "raw deal" from every angle. Jacob lied and cheated and connived him out of what was rightfully his. He could not please his father altogether, and his mother could not stand him, yet he longed for approval as much as any child possibly could.

Remember, the subject is still understanding your child —knowing your child. Take some time with your child. Understand him. Learn what he is thinking, and see if you have become partial to one of your children. Do not ever think that this is an impossibility.

I recently talked with a man who has a real problem in his family. He said, "I know what the problem is. My little girl is just like me. She is full of the devil, she is hot tempered, you can't tell her anything. . ." and on and on he went. He said. "My little boy, though, is the sweetest thing. I try to embrace my daughter, and she is just as apt to kick me as not. But my little boy runs to me and throws his arms around me." And he said, "I find myself saying, 'Mary, I wish you were more like Jim.' " Finally he said, "I just don't know what the answer is." I pointed out this passage in the Word of God, because I believe that therein lies the answer. It was all based on the child's desire for approval. Notice what Esau did, as recorded in Genesis 28:6-9:

> 6 When Esau saw that Isaac had blessed Jacob, and sent him away to Padan-aram, to take him a wife from thence; and that as he blessed him he gave him a charge, saying, Thou shalt not take a wife of the daughters of Canaan;
> 7 And that Jacob obeyed his father and his mother, and was gone to Padan-aram;
> 8 And Esau seeing that the daughters of Canaan pleased not Isaac his father;
> 9 Then went Esau unto Ishmael, and took unto the wives which he had Mahalath the daughter of Ishmael Abraham's son, the sister of Nebajoth, to be his wife.

Do you see what he did? He listened to Isaac tell Jacob to go get a wife from back home, instead of getting one from Canaan. I am quite sure, even though the record does not state it, that Isaac said, "Now, Jacob, if you marry a girl like those that Esau married, it will be the death of your mother. She has not said much to you, but she has kept me awake at night telling me about it. Her nerves are shot. We would have to put her away if you married one of those girls." And away Jacob went, to tell her the whole story.

Perhaps Esau was nearby, heard the conversation, and got to thinking about it. "I wish Mother would love me. I wish Dad really loved me. What can I do to gain their approval?" Then a thought struck him. "That's it! They do not like these wives that I got from Canaan. I will marry one of the daughters of Ishmael, too." So he went down and made a quick marriage with one of the daughters of Ishmael, hoping to gain his parents' approval.

But did you notice, there is not one suggestion that Esau was ever approved. The Bible says that God loved Jacob and hated

Esau, and that is a statement that has bothered a lot of people. It is a relative statement; among other things it means that there were some things in the life of Jacob that caused God to love him, and some things in the life of Esau that caused God to disapprove of him. I think, on the basis of our discussion, that those things were not entirely the fault of Esau. I think they were also the fault of his parents and his grandparents. If they had understood their children as they should have, and had watched for these indications, things might have been greatly different.

In chapter 12 of the Book of Hebrews there is another comment about Esau. It is that Esau was a "profane" man. That does not mean that he took the Lord's name in vain; it means that he had trouble with the flesh. It means that he fought a constant battle with the flesh. As we have seen, there were many unbecoming aspects of Jacob's character. Nevertheless, if you will read the entire history of the life of Jacob, you will discover this about him: He always had a spiritual proclivity, he had a desire for spiritual things that Esau did not have.

Perhaps you have heard the statement, "It is just easy for some people to be good." You may have dismissed that as being untrue, but it is true. There are some people who are born with inclinations and desires toward spiritual things, and others whose desires toward fleshly things make their walk with the Lord a constant battle.

If you have more than one child in your family, watch closely, and you may find one of your children seemingly readily obedient and another one bowing his neck every time he gets a chance. You may find one child interested in spiritual things and another child fighting a real battle in relation to spiritual things. It will be a matter not of his wish, but of a tremendous pull against him.

If you find that one of your children is rebellious, don't talk about how you wish he were obedient like your other child. Do not say anything. Get on your knees first of all, and ask God to give you wisdom. Ask Him to give you understanding of that child. Then deal with the child as you need to deal with a rebellious child, recognizing that there is a possibility that he has a deeper desire than your other child to do what you want him to do, but his nature is such that it is difficult for him to do it. His nature is such, first of all, because of Adam's sin, and secondly, because of the nature that he has inherited from you.

There are some applications here that could be easily misunderstood and therefore require careful thought. I am often asked what I think about the adoption of children. My answer always is this: "If I were you, I would pray about it very earnestly. I would be sure that the Lord wanted me to do it. I would not do it just because my heart was touched by a homeless little child. I would be very sure that the Lord wanted me to do it, because you could get into some very real problems."

Invariably, almost defensively, they come back with the reply, "Well, don't you have any problems with your children?" I say, "Yes, I do, but I know where those problems came from. Every time I hear one of my children tell a lie, I know that it is because I am basically a liar, were it not for the grace of God. Every time I see one of my children bowing his neck and having a temper tantrum, even though it gets interrupted before it gets very far along, I know why; I can see in my children the ungodly temper I was born with."

If you have an adopted child you have a greater responsibility than the average and a harder job to understand that child. You will not have the advantage of seeing yourself in him. You will have to wait on the Lord—not talk it out before the child, but wait on the Lord—and say, "Lord, why is he acting this way? Give me wisdom to understand, so I won't say or do the wrong thing."

Please do not get the impression that adopted children cannot be properly reared by adoptive parents, because they can. There are many very precious adopted children who have been reared in such a way that God has been able to use them abundantly. This is merely an application.

Study your child, know your child, and recognize that the thing you must use as a guidepost is the problem that great-great-grandfather started three generations ago. It will crop out in a dozen different ways, and you need to recognize it.

3

God's Plan for Your Child

Proverbs 22:6 can be discussed from different standpoints. We want now to discuss it from the standpoint of the good that is implied. This verse, coupled with other verses of Scripture, teaches that God has a plan for every child that is born into the world, and that He puts within the personality of that child the elements that will aid in the pursuit of the plan that God has for him. There is Scripture to support this. It boils down to the simple fact that instead of sending your child to a testing center to have an aptitude test to find out what he is suited for, you should spend some time with the Lord in a study of your child to find out what he is fitted for.

I had a conference recently with an engineer who is as miserable as he can be. He is a success, he has a good job, and he is making a handsome salary. But he is absolutely miserable. He hates his work with a bitter passion. I said, "Why? Why, with life as brief as it is, are you spending all of your time in something that you hate so bitterly?" He said, "It is the only thing that I am fitted for." I asked, "Who said so?" He mentioned a well-known school that specializes in giving tests to determine fitness for various occupations.

He said, "When I was in my first year of college, I did not know what I should study, so I went to this school and took the test. I am fitted to be an engineer. That is what the test showed. So I became an engineer. I hate the work, but I am fitted for it."

I pointed out to him from the Word of God that God has a purpose for every person born into the world. If we as parents do not help our children find out what that purpose is, we may have some really unhappy personalities to deal with before it is over. Above all else, remember this: The purpose that God has for your children is not necessarily the purpose you have for them.

We have seen thus far that every child, including your child, is bent in a threefold way. He is bent first of all toward evil in a general sense. You must understand that. If you ask yourself why your child does a certain undesirable thing, the answer is that it is his bent. We are speaking of training your child with the understanding that his natural inclination is to do bad instead of good, and of making provision for that inclination.

We have seen also that this inclination is first, in a general sense, and second, in a specific sense. Not only are all people born into the world with the nature of Adam, but as we have suggested, all people are born into the world with the problems that great-great-grandfather started. You may be reaping in your child today the harvest of the seeds that his great-great-grandfather sowed, and you must keep that in mind in your training.

The third thing that we have said about the bent of the child is what we want to consider now, and it is that they are bent in a good sense. Not only is the bent toward evil, but when God was bending the bow, He was bending it in a good sense as well. We should notice that, because this is where the responsibility comes in. Most of us are guilty of sins of omission as well as sins of commission, and this is especially true in regard to our children. Many of us reproach ourselves for the mistakes we have made in rearing our children. We say to ourselves, "If we had not done this or that, perhaps he would not have done that terrible thing that he did." But it is also important to recognize the sins of omission in this relationship—not the things we do, but the things we fail to do because we do not understand our children. If we understand them, we will not omit these things.

Psalm 139 has some important thoughts along these lines. The first five verses of the psalm deal with the omniscience of God. The word *omniscience* means that God knows all; He has knowledge of everything. Those first five verses tell us that God knows everything there is to know about us. The psalmist's reaction to this is given in verse 6, where he says just about what you and I would say: "Such knowledge is too wonderful for me, and I cannot begin to understand it.'' I think you will agree with me that we cannot understand how God knows so much about us as individuals when there are so many other individuals in the world—how He knows our downsitting and our uprising. That is pretty particular knowledge, but the Bible says it, and we must believe it.

This passage of Scripture also says that He knows our thoughts before we are able to formulate them. He knows my words even before I say them.

The paragraph that begins with verse 7 and concludes with verse 12 speaks of the omnipresence of God, which means that God is everywhere. The psalmist suggests the various places where he goes and says that God is there. If you do not read the passage carefully, this might strike fear to your heart, but that is contrary to the theme of the psalm. It should be a great assurance to read these verses, for the psalmist is not suggesting that he is trying to run away from God. He is saying, rather, that no matter where he is, God is there—that God never leaves him alone. If he is in the darkest place, the darkness becomes light because God is there.

The reason for this knowledge on the part of God and the purpose of God's presence with those who are His own comprise the subject for our present discussion. In the first twelve verses, the theme followed by the psalmist is: ''Why should God be so interested in me that everywhere I am, He is—that He never leaves me lonely?'' The answer is given in verse 13:

> For thou hast possessed my reins: thou hast covered me in my mother's womb.

In a very general sense, this verse says that God is interested in us to this extent because He was interested in us from the very moment of our conception. So why shouldn't He be interested in us now?

Just for the sake of clarification of a somewhat technical point, we should realize that the Word of God indicates that He was interested in us even before we were conceived. If you do not understand that, do not be surprised. I do not know of anyone who with his finite mind can grasp an infinite truth like that. But if we believe the Word of God we cannot reject certain parts of it simply because our inadequate minds cannot comprehend how it could be possible.

For the purposes of our discussion, then, let us settle in our minds that God was interested in us from the moment of conception, until birth, and afterwards. Since we are thinking about children, let me suggest that God was interested in your child the moment he was conceived. It certainly would be good if we could be interested in our children from that moment. Most of us wait until our children are born and then we get interested. Many of us wait until they get a little older and begin to present problems, and then we get interested. God was interested in our children from the moment they were conceived. Verse 13 makes this very clear.

The verse may not mean very much to you the way it is written. So the best thing to do is to look at the individual words in the verse and on this basis determine what it actually says.

Notice the word "possessed" to begin with. It is a translation of a Hebrew word that speaks of erecting a building, or of some particular thing that is being formed or built. We might read the verse this way: "Thou hast formed, or built, my reins. . . ."

Then look at the word "reins." What does it mean? Any number of pictures may come to your mind, because it is not a word that we use in this way today, and it is not a word that expresses the thought of this verse as accurately as it should.

If you are familiar with languages, particularly Hebrew or Greek, you know that these languages have a way of amplifying the meaning of words. When this word first began to be used, it referred to an organ that was created for some particular purpose. Later it was used to refer generally to the vital organs of the body, and it is those organs that are under discussion in this verse. If you look at the verse with that thought in mind, you might read it this way: "For thou hast formed my vital organs. . . ." No, nature did not form those organs; God did it.

Notice also in this verse the word "covered" in the phrase "Thou hast covered me in my mother's womb." This is a translation of a Hebrew word that means "to join" or "to knit together," just as bones are knit or sinews are joined together. The verse as we read it says, "Thou hast possessed my reins: thou hast covered me in my mother's womb," but in the light of the meanings of these words, what it actually says is, "Thou hast formed my particular vital organs, such as my kidneys; thou hast knitted, or joined, me together."

Do you see now why we make the statement that God should be interested in us in this life? He was interested in us from the moment of conception.

When David realized that God had created him with great care for the vital organs of his body, he said in verse 14:

> I will praise thee; for I am fearfully and wonderfully made: marvellous are thy works; and that my soul knoweth right well.

Look at verse 15, because there he is continuing the discussion of verse 13 (verse 14 is simply a note of praise):

> My substance was not hid from thee, when I was made in secret, and curiously wrought in the lowest parts of the earth.

That has a little more meaning than the previous verse, but it is still not as clear as it might be. The word "substance" in our English text is a very general word, but that is not true of the word used in the original. The Hebrew word refers to the bony structure of the body. You might even use the word "skeleton" if you prefer.

What is he saying here? "My bony structure, my skeleton, was not hid from thee when I was made in secret and curiously wrought in the lowest parts of the earth." We will understand better what this word "hid" means when we come to the next verse, so just pass over it for a moment. Look at the word "made": "My skeleton was not hid from thee when I was made." That is a very interesting word. It is the same word that is used in the Book of Genesis when the Scripture says that God formed the earth. It is a translation of the Hebrew word *asah,* and it refers to making something out of that which already exists. It is important to remember this meaning, because the word "made" in the Scripture is not always a translation of that word. Sometimes the words "made" or "created" or "formed" in the Scripture are translations of the Hebrew word that means to create something out of matter that has never before been in existence. But in this instance the idea is that the skeleton was created out of substances already in existence. So the use of the Hebrew word *asah* is accurate to the last degree; this allows for the laws of heredity in relation to the formation of your child. The meaning of the verse is: "My skeleton was not hid from thee when I was made from substances already in existence.''

Look at another word in that verse, "secret," which is not a very happy translation. It is a translation of a Hebrew word that describes a protected place, such as the womb. Why does God place the embryo in the womb of the mother? Why does He protect it in the fashion that He does? That the child may be safely cared for until it is brought to birth. So when you read the word "secret" here, it is not a suggestion of something that is done in hiding; it is a word that describes a protected place, such as the womb of a mother.

Then notice the phrase "the lowest parts of the earth." That is an idiom. Actually, what it is saying is, "when I was made in a protected place, such as the lowest part of the earth." If you want to protect something, one way to do it is to dig a hole and bury it. That is the comparison here.

There is another phrase in the verse that is exceedingly important; it is the phrase "curiously wrought." It is a translation of one Hebrew word that describes a number of things which are related but different. For example, this is the word that is translated "embroidery." When we are told in the Old Testament that the curtains of the temple were embroidered, this is the word that is used. It is also used to describe needlepoint—fine, varicolored, variegated work. It is also translated "fabricate."

When we put all the meanings of all these words together, we might read the verse in this way: "My skeleton was not hid from thee when I was created out of existing material, as protected in the womb as if I were in the depths of the earth, and fabricated as intricately as embroidery of different colors, and fine needlepoint."

Look at verse 16, because David is continuing the same subject:

> Thine eyes did see my substance, yet being unperfect; and in thy book all my members were written, which in continuance were fashioned, when as yet there was none of them.

Notice the word "substance." This is not the same Hebrew word that was used in verse 15. As a matter of fact, a phrase in this verse, "my substance, yet being unperfect," is a translation of one Hebrew word that can be translated "embryo." Do you see the difference? In verse 15 the word "substance" refers to the skeleton or bony framework of the body, but in verse 16 the word "substance" refers to the embryo from which the body actually grows.

Then notice the phrase "in thy book all my members were written, which in continuance were fashioned, when as yet there was none of them." The word translated "continuance" is from a Hebrew word that has presented problems in translation, and there are some alternate translations. Actually it is a word that means "the hot hours of the day." It is a reference to the hours of the day in which work can be done.

The King James Version translates this word as "continuance," referring to the hours of the day in which work can be done, because the word "continuance" also means "day." An alternate translation is something like this: "Thine eyes did see my substance, yet being unperfect, and in thy book all my days are written." Both of those truths are in this one passage of Scripture.

We will look at it first as it is presented in the King James text. You will notice that the words "my members" are in italics, meaning that they were not in the original text. This translation, however, is exactly right, because the original text has only the word "all." The person who is reading, or who is hearing, will relate this word "all" to the subject under discussion. Actually the word "all" in itself could refer to anything.

What are we talking about here? We are talking about the body, are we not? We are talking about the vital organs of the body. We are talking about the bony framework of the body. So it is quite in keeping with the original meaning of the word to say, "Thine eyes did see the embryo of my being, and in thy book all my members are written."

The word translated "written" in this verse could be better translated "described." It is as though a man wrote down in a book the thing that he was going to do before he ever did it, as though he described it in detail.

Here is something that we have to accept by faith: God writes down, in the book of His plan for every man's life, the kind of individual that person is going to be. That is what this Scripture says: God writes down whether he will be tall or short, whether he will be born with every member of his body complete or incomplete—whether he will be born perfect, as we say, though that is a relative term in this day in which we live—or whether he will be born with some affliction. God knows all that about every individual who is born.

That becomes even more evident if you will look at the word "see," because this is not a word that describes ordinary looking. It is a word, rather, that describes watching over a certain thing that is being done, with a great deal of care to see that it is done right.

Earlier, in verse 15, when he said, "My substance was not hid from thee," that was just what he meant. God was not off somewhere doing something else, and just let a child be planted in a mother's womb, and then be born in whatever way it would be born. As far as God is concerned, there is no such thing as an "accident of nature." There is no such thing as a thing just happening. If this passage of Scripture is true, God has written down in His book a plan for every individual's life and the kind of person that individual is going to be, even in his physical body.

That is additionally shown to be true if you will look at verse 16. The word "fashioned" in that verse is a translation of a Hebrew word that speaks of something's being molded and formed into shape. It is a word that describes a potter as he takes a piece of clay and molds it into something new. That is why you read in the last part of this verse, "when as yet there was none of them." Actually, this phrase is not in the original text. It is an amplification of one Hebrew word that means to fashion something that has not yet been in existence.

If we read verse 16, paraphrasing it in the light of these words we have suggested, it would be something like this: "Thine eyes did watch over my embryo, and all my members were described in thy book in that day before they were formed."

We have been thinking about the sense of this passage of Scripture, and now we would like to think about some of the lessons that can be learned from it.

Let us look at verse 13 and some of the things it suggests. The text says, "For thou hast possessed my reins; thou hast covered me in my mother's womb." The suggested translation was "For thou hast formed my vital organs, thou hast knitted, or joined, me together.'' Verse 16 should be included, because the verses go together. ''Thine eyes did watch over my embryo, and all of the parts of my body were described in thy book in that day before they were formed.''

If these verses mean anything at all, they mean that from the time the child is conceived until the time it is born, God is watching over the process of growth. This ''watching over'' could be compared to an architect's watching over the construction of a building to insure that all the specifications are met.

One of the implications of this idea can be a source of real comfort to our hearts. It is that God is watching over the birth of every child that is born into the world. He is watching over the formation of that child, and if that child is born in what we refer to as an afflicted condition, it comes as no surprise to God. We do not need to go around wondering why it happened. We do not need to go around reproaching ourselves for what happened. We can rest in the fact that God knew what was happening.

A natural question is, ''Why would He let a thing like that happen if He knew all about it?'' In answer to that, there are two things that must be kept in mind. The first of these is that we do not look upon things as God looks upon them. In the minds of most parents, one of the worst things that could happen would be to give birth to an afflicted child. But that may not be the worst thing from God's viewpoint. It could be the best thing that could ever have happened were we able to see the overall picture, and not just the immediate.

There are two possible attitudes to the birth of afflicted children. One of them is as wrong as it can be, but the other strikes a happy medium. These two attitudes are presented in a little story in John 9. In verse 1 the story is introduced:

And as Jesus passed by, he saw a man which was blind from his birth.

Stop and think about that. Here was a man who was born blind. Immediately the question comes to people's minds, ''Why? Why was that child born blind?'' One commonly held opinion is expressed in verse 2:

And his disciples asked him, saying, Master, who did sin,

this man, or his parents, that he was born blind?

That is an attitude that many, many people have. If a child is born in an afflicted condition, then God is judging the parents or He is judging the child. But that is completely erroneous. The Lord Jesus Christ answered that immediately by saying in verse 3:

. . . Neither hath this man sinned, nor his parents. . . .

We must not think, when afflicted children are born into the world, that they are born in that condition as God's judgment against the parents or against the child.

What is the other attitude? Look at the last part of verse 3:

. . . but that the works of God should be made manifest in him.

Most people stop right there. They have the wrong opinion of God. They say, "God let that child be afflicted just so He could get some glory." But that is not the case. You have to read on. You must remember that there are no punctuation marks in the Greek text, so let me suggest punctuation that presents a correct image of God. The Lord came to the end of a thought in the middle of verse 3, and then He said:

. . . but that the works of God should be made manifest in him. I must work the works of him that sent me, while it is day: the night cometh, when no man can work.

When an afflicted child is born into a family and God is given a chance to work, it can be a source of great blessing to that family, a source of blessing to the whole world, and a channel of great glory to God. The parents of Helen Keller could have done what many parents have done with their afflicted children—put her in a back room somewhere and not let anybody see her; they could have reproached themselves for the rest of their lives because their child was afflicted. Instead, they took an attitude that was ahead of their generation by many, many years. They considered the child an exceptional one—exceptional in the sense that she presented a great opportunity for God to work. And He certainly did.

Perhaps you have read Dale Evan's book *Angel Unaware*. It is a simple book, but it has a message. When an afflicted child was born into that family, people felt so sorry. But Dale Evans Rogers had the right attitude: This was an angel, even though people did not realize it. We are not thinking of a literal angel, but of a blessing, a thing that is precious.

That is the attitude that God expects every one of us to take about an afflicted child. It is never an accident when a child is born that way. God has been watching over it. He could have prevented it, but He permitted it for a special purpose.

The second thing that must be kept in mind in regard to afflicted children is suggested by the use of the word "made" in Psalm 139, verse 15. As has already been suggested, it is a word that speaks of making something out of that which is already in existence.

One of the things suggested by the use of this word is that when God forms a child in its mother's womb, He forms it out of material that is already in existence. That material is made available through the father and mother, and many of the times when people are distressed with God because their baby is not perfect, they should actually be distressed with themselves. Not in the sense that God is punishing them for some sin, but in the sense that God has set nature in order, and He operátes along certain lines. He never overrules the laws of nature unless there is a specific reason for it. You and I cannot live carelessly and then expect God to overrule the laws of nature just to permit us to have a child that is above and beyond our expectations. After a woman becomes pregnant, she should read this passage of Scripture and be conscientious about the way she lives while that child is being formed.

We will not go into a medical discussion here, but if we would, it could be well established that some children are born in the condition in which they are born because the mother did not think enough of the holy privilege of giving birth to a child to curtail certain of her activities while she was carrying the child. God does limit Himself to creating children out of the material that is already there.

All of the things suggested in these two verses have been a great comfort to my own heart in regard to the problem of afflicted children. They have also been a comfort in regard to the problem of miscarriage. My wife once had a miscarriage. We have seven children and would have had an eighth. We were as grieved over that miscarriage as we would have been if one of our children had died. It was another life that might have been entrusted to our care to do something for God. We have gained great comfort from this passage of Scripture, knowing that God was watching over the formation of the child. Some time later it was revealed through medical evaluation that the condition of my wife's womb was such that no child could have lived for long in that womb. If by some strange chance, the doctors said, the child had been born, it would not have been anything but a vegetable.

It is a great comfort to know that God knows which children to bring to birth, and He knows in what condition they will be born. We can leave these things with Him, and not be worried or reproachful of ourselves.

Perhaps you are wondering what all this has to do with child training. Well, it is basic. God has been good to my wife and me in that all of our seven children are perfect physically, by the grace of God. None of them is afflicted, as we commonly use that term. But had one been, what would have been our attitude? How would we have trained such a child? How we would have discharged our responsibility comes right back to this matter of knowing your child. We would have to know how God formed him in the womb and the purpose for which He formed him.

Let us amplify this a little more, on a brighter side. Our paraphrased translation of verse 15 was: "My skeleton was not hid from thee when I was created out of existing material, as protected in the womb as if I were in the depths of the earth, and fabricated as intricately as embroidery of different colors, and fine needlepoint."

It is not true, regardless of what you have heard, that all men are created equal. They are not. We should thank God that we live in a country where we have equal opportunities, but we are not all created equal, and it is a great mistake to think we are. One of the basic things we need to remember in training our children is that our children are not necessarily equal to all the other children they know. One of the gravest mistakes that parents make is to assume that their child ought to be able to do something that some other child does.

Each child, as he is formed by God in his mother's womb, is formed with as much care as that with which an artist might embroider a piece of cloth, or as a woman might very beautifully, but very tediously, create a piece of needlepoint. Such pieces of art would not all be the same. They would not all have the same colors, they would not all look the same, and we would not expect them to.

From time to time I have had to deal with children who are nervous wrecks because their parents pushed them too hard. Such parents assume that just because other children are brilliant, their child should be, too. It does not necessarily follow that he is. I have seen young people completely frustrated because their parents assumed that they had talents that the young people themselves knew well they did not have.

You see, this verse of Scripture deals not only with the general creation of man with regard to the vital organs that we all have, but it also deals with what we commonly refer to as "talents." God in His wisdom has given every child certain abilities and talents that can ultimately be used for His glory. Not every child has the same gifts that every other child has. It would be wise for us to study our children and see what kind of embroidery God used, and then act accordingly. As has been suggested, some of us as parents will have to answer to God for failing to realize that He did implant within our children certain talents which, for any number of reasons, we have ignored.

For example, God implants musical talents within some children. He also implants other talents, but there is a Scriptural reference to musical talents. In Ezekiel 28 there is a passage of Scripture that deals with one of God's created beings. Just because he was not human, in the sense that we commonly think of it, is no reason to assume that he was created in any other manner than were all of God's other creatures. Here is a picture of the devil before he became the devil—a picture of Satan when he was at the height of all God's creation, the most beautiful and most talented of all God's creatures:

> 11 Moreover the word of the Lord came unto me, saying,
> 12 Son of man, take up a lamentation upon the king of Tyrus, and say unto him, thus saith the Lord God; thou sealest up the sum, full of wisdom, and perfect in beauty.

That means that Satan was the wisest and most beautiful of all of God's creatures. You may be wondering why he was addressed as the king of Tyrus (Tyre). God often does this. He addresses in the name of an individual the one who is prompting that individual. For example, when Peter said to the Lord Jesus Christ, in speaking of His crucifixion, "Lord, You are not going to die on the cross," the Lord did not say, "Get behind me, Peter"; He said, "Get behind me, Satan" (Matt. 16:23). He knew that Satan had prompted Peter to say that.

The king of Tyrus is described in the first ten verses of this chapter. God talks to him; then He goes beyond the king of Tyrus and talks to the creature who is prompting him. He said in verse 12, "You are the most beautiful, and you are the wisest." In verse 13 He said, "You have been in Eden, the garden of God, and every precious stone was your covering," and He names the stones. What that verse means literally is that Satan lived in a place made of precious stones in the Garden of Eden.

The next phrase, in verse 13, is the one in which we are particularly interested:

... the workmanship of thy tabrets and of thy pipes was prepared in thee in the day that thou wast created. ...

The Book of Job tells us that before this angelic being became the devil, the sons of God sang together. That must have been a beautiful sound! We are told that Satan led them in their singing, for he was not only the wisest and most beautiful, but he was also the most talented of all the sons of God. God created in him this musical ability, as is indicated by the mention of "tabrets" and "pipes," both of which are musical instruments.

We could go on and think about all the varied talents God creates in children before He permits them to be born into the world. But the purpose of the illustration is to show that it is exceedingly important for you as a parent to study your child and find out what his talents are. Give him the opportunity to develop those talents.

A very important application of the truth of these verses is related to discipline. You may find, if you have not already done so, that some of your discipline problems are the result of a child's being thwarted in the pursuit of his God-given talents. He may not know that; all he may know is that he feels frustrated. You may know that he feels frustrated and thwarted and miserable and you cannot live with him, but you do not know why. But if you had taken the time to study him, you might have found that the talent

God gave him and with which he is literally "bursting at the seams" is being neglected.

Some parents neglect their children's talents because they do not think they are important. For example, there may be a so-called "outdoor man," and his son may have a talent for music. The father may say to himself, "I will die before I will let my son play the piano." Well, this son may wish he could die, too, because of the difference in personality. If the child does have that talent, it should be developed. There may be a child with an artistic talent, and a very practical father may say, "I am not going to fool with that. An artist would starve to death." He may thwart the child's talent because of an economic concern.

Others say, "I am not going to let him pursue this talent because we just can't afford it. All God expects me to do is to feed and clothe him." That is not all that God expects you to do. He expects you to study your child and to know positively what that child is capable of doing. Then you are to act in that direction.

It should be stressed again that not all the children in your family will be the same. One of the greatest mistakes you can make is to try to make one of your children measure up to another of your children, or to give one of your children the idea that you are more interested in the activities that another of the children is pursuing than in the activities that he is pursuing. Discipline is related to this.

Sometimes you wonder why a child embarrasses you every time he gets a chance. You just cannot understand it, after all you have told him. Just let a group of people come in, and there he goes, and you do not know why. If you would stop to analyze it, you might find that it is related to this subject. You have not taken the time to study your child, to see what his capabilities are and to let him use those capabilities to the fullest extent. And perhaps you have not taken into consideration, if you have more than one child, that not all your children are the same.

God has been good to us. He has given my wife and me five girls and two boys. God has given us the privilege of living with daughters who differ from one another even physically. He gave us a blonde, a brunette, and a redhead, and you cannot beat that. They have different personalities, too. On top of that, he gave us a set of twin girls, and you cannot compare that, because it is an absolutely new experience, different from anything else. He gave us two boys, one seven years older than the other, and there is a real difference in them, too.

We would be making a great mistake if we should try to make them all do the same thing, all act the same way, and all wear the same clothes. Of course, we do not. We ask God to give us wisdom in regard to each one, and we ask Him to give us understanding about their talents, and we encourage them as much as we can.

Our oldest daughter has some musical talent. When we first discovered her talent, we left no stone unturned to let her develop it. From an economic standpoint and from a time standpoint, we did not hold her back. That is a talent God gave her, and she needed to develop it with our encouragement.

We have another daughter who has some real artistic talent. I am quite sure that the average person would say that it is foolish to spend money on paints, canvas, and so forth, but we do not think that. We think we will be responsible to God if she fails to develop the talent that God gave her.

Another of our daughters has a real talent for making clothes. I feel certain that she does not need all the dresses she makes, but she needs to develop her talent. With us it is a matter of not neglecting the talent that God gave her.

It might prove to be embarrassing to encourage the development of a talent; there was a time when our youngest son's greatest talent seemed to be for playing bongo drums! During that time I diligently tried to discover some way to direct all that rhythm into a more profitable area!

4

The First Step

A primary question that presents itself at this point in our discussion must be: "How shall I know in which direction my child is bent?" We have spent quite a bit of time emphasizing that it is our responsibility as parents to understand which way the child is bent and to train him accordingly. So the question naturally arises, "How can we know the direction of his bent?" We want to examine that matter now.

The first and basic step in understanding a child is to recognize what that child means to God. If we are to recognize which way a child is bent, we need to understand that in God's sight children are the most important creatures in the world. Only as we recognize that fact will we have the correct attitude in training our children according to their predetermined course in life.

If your children are just a "necessary evil," you will never be able to do it. But if you realize that, as far as God is concerned, the most important creature in the world is a child, you will be able to train your child as God has ordered. For us to realize that, we will have to recognize what the Bible says about the birth of children, and we may have to rid ourselves of some ideas that we already hold.

God has ordained the process whereby children are conceived and brought into the world. It would seem, if we leave the Word of God out of it for a moment, that if all the conditions are met, the birth of children is inevitable. It would also seem, since the birth of children occurs at inopportune times and places and under inopportune conditions, that all that childbirth amounts to is the planting of the seed and the growth of the individual. We do recognize that children are born to unwed mothers, and with our human outlook it is hard for us to understand that. We recognize that children are born into homes and under conditions that are less than desirable, and with our finite minds it is hard for us to understand the wisdom of that. So we jump to the conclusion that the birth of children is due solely to a biological process that begins and ends in a certain fashion. If, however, we inject the Word of God into the situation, and recognize that the Word of God is the inspired message of God to us, then we will have to recognize that God rules and overrules in the birth of children. We need to keep in mind that though some of these births seem unwise to us, we cannot see as God can see, and therefore the way we feel is not necessarily the way God feels.

A number of verses of Scripture verify that God is sovereign in regard to the birth of children. There are a number of passages of Scripture that tell us that God shuts up the womb or that God opens the womb—that God makes possible the birth of children or that God sometimes refuses to permit children to be born.

One such passage is Genesis, chapter 20. Keep in mind that these are not local suggestions related to people who felt differently about children from the way we do in the twentieth century. If the Holy Spirit is the author of the Bible, and He is, then certainly these are timeless principles that are enunciated, and not just local situations. This chapter tells the story of Abimelech, king of Egypt, who took Abraham's wife into his own harem, and it displeased God. We read that God told Abimelech that he would have to let Sarah go back to Abraham or a curse, which He had placed upon the wives of Abimelech, would not be lifted. That is a summary of the chapter. We are interested in the last two verses:

> 17 So Abraham prayed unto God: and God healed Abimelech, and his wife, and his maidservants; and they bare children.
> 18 For the Lord had fast closed up all the wombs of the house of Abimelech, because of Sarah Abraham's wife.

Here is a definite statement that God closed up the wombs of the women in the royal harem because Abimelech displeased God.

Before we jump to conclusions, let me emphasize that when God closes the womb of a woman it is not always a punishment. It is not always because God is displeased. Sometimes it is due to no other reason than the physical condition of the woman involved. It does not indicate pleasure or displeasure on the part of God. But this is a fact that we want to establish: God is able to shut up or open the womb.

Another passage dealing with the subject is Genesis 29. Although we are not interested in the details other than the sovereign right of God to open and close wombs, the background is essential to the understanding of verse 31. This is the story of Leah and Rachel. Jacob was deceived into marrying Leah first before he could marry Rachel, the girl he really loved. In later years he was very partial to Rachel. Out of sympathy for Leah, God evened up the situation:

> 31 And when the Lord saw that Leah was hated, he opened her womb: but Rachel was barren.

Look at Genesis 30:22, which tells how it developed later:

> 22 And God remembered Rachel, and God hearkened to her, and opened her womb.

There was a time when God closed the womb of Rachel and nothing opened it—not even some superstitious practices of the day.

In these instances there were different reasons for the opening and the closing of the womb by God. We are emphasizing the fact that God had different reasons for showing that He is sovereign in the birth of children; birth is not due solely to a biological process. We find in Scripture also the story of Elkanah and his wife Hannah. I Samuel 1:4-5 records the story:

> 4 And when the time was that Elkanah offered, he gave to Peninnah his wife, and to all her sons and her daughters, portions:
> 5 But unto Hannah he gave a worthy portion; for he loved Hannah: but the Lord had shut up her womb.

Here is another instance where a womb was closed. If you were to follow the story of her life, you would find that Hannah was very godly. She lived very close to God, and, still, God closed up her womb. This is emphasized so that no one will think that the lack of children is always an indication that God is displeased. It is not. God may close the womb for various reasons.

Let us notice Psalm 113, which is devoted to praise of God for what He is able to do. In verse 9 there is a statement along the line we are considering:

> He maketh the barren woman to keep house, and to be a joyful mother of children.

Here is a definite statement, one that needs no elaboration, that God is able to bring children into the world or to keep them out of the world, as it seems good to Him.

If we keep in mind that God is sovereign in the birth of children, we will have to realize that the birth of children is a special blessing from the Lord. That is one of the reasons for emphasizing God's sovereignty. If God permits children to be born into the world, it is not a mere result of a biological process; it is according to the plan and purpose of God. Children are so important in God's sight that when He entrusts us as human beings with children, He could confer upon us no greater honor; they are most important in the realm of God's creation.

We should notice this from the Word of God. Psalm 127 is a good starting point. Sometimes a psalm like this brings a bit of humor to our minds, because the language suggests a humorous thought or two. But we need to keep in mind that these words were written by inspiration, and they portray exactly how God feels about children:

> 3 Lo, children are an heritage of the Lord: and the fruit of the womb is his reward.
> 4 As arrows are in the hand of a mighty man; so are children of the youth.
> 5 Happy is the man that hath his quiver full of them: they shall not be ashamed, but they shall speak with the enemies in the gate.

Notice that children are a heritage of the Lord and the fruit of the womb and that children are His reward to man. Let us not misconstrue that verse. It does not say that God gives you a child as a special reward for being good. It says that God gives you a child, and that child in itself is the reward of living. It is what makes life purposeful. It is what makes life have meaning. That is why it is said in the next verse that as arrows are in the hand of a mighty man, so are the children of youth. It is a suggestion that as you aim the arrow, so will it fly. You can have no greater instrument for good than the child that is trained at your knee. Thus the Word of God says, "Happy is the man who has his quiver full of them."

Incidentally, not everybody's quiver is the same size. There is no need to think that a very large family is what we are talking about here. It may be large, but it does not necessarily follow that it must be, because not every man's quiver is the same size. Only as God fills the quiver, and you recognize that these children are arrows in your hand, does the effectiveness of this passage of Scripture become clear. Notice the words of Psalm 128:

1 Blessed is every one that feareth the Lord, that walketh in his ways.
2 For thou shalt eat the labour of thine hands: happy shalt thou be, and it shall be well with thee.
3 Thy wife shall be as a fruitful vine by the sides of thine house: thy children like olive plants round about thy table.
4 Behold, that thus shall the man be blessed that feareth the Lord.
5 The Lord shall bless thee out of Zion: and thou shalt see the good of Jerusalem all the days of thy life.
6 Yea, thou shalt see thy children's children, and peace upon Israel.

Particularly in verses 3 and 4, we are told that the man who walks in the will of God and fears God is a man who will be trusted by God with children in his home. Some people are inclined to disannul this passage of Scripture; they say, "Oh, that was in the Old Testament, when they believed in big families." If you say that, you will have to say that it belongs only to the Old Testament for a man to enjoy the fruit of the labor of his hands, because it is in this same Old Testament psalm. If you say that large families belong only to the Old Testament, then you will also have to say that the man who works hard today has no right to enjoy what he earns.

These verses of Scripture should emphasize to our hearts that God is sovereign in the birth of children. If we accept the Word of God at its face value, we will recognize that children are a heritage from the Lord; they are a special blessing from God, which He entrusts to us. When we have realized this, mothers will be less likely to look upon their children as a handicap that forced them to quit the job they enjoyed so they could rear the children. They will be less likely to look upon them as a burden on the budget; you know, "We were doing so well until we found out we were going to have this other child; now it has upset the budget. . . ." We won't look upon these children as a hindrance to our social pleasure. We will look upon them, rather, in a twofold way that is suggested in the Word of God. We will look upon them first of all with a fear of the awesome responsibility we have as parents, and then we will look upon them as a source of the greatest pleasure that life can afford.

The Lord Jesus Christ used a little child as an object lesson in Matthew 18. We are familiar with some of what He said, because it is often emphasized:

> 3 Verily I say unto you, Except ye be converted, and become as little children, ye shall not enter into the kingdom of heaven.

That is true. But because that verse comes first, we are inclined to interpret all the rest of the paragraph in the light of that one verse. In doing so we miss its full import:

> 5 And whoso shall receive one such little child in my name receiveth me.

Because of verse 3, we usually interpret this to mean being kind to little children and being sure they get to Sunday school. That is fine. But this is actually a broader statement than that. If you receive a child that is born into your home as a direct gift from God, you will be receiving the Lord Jesus Christ into your home, figuratively speaking. That is the essence of this verse.

Just for the sake of discussion, suppose you had a special message from heaven that Jesus Christ was to visit your home tomorrow. You really believed the message and were convinced it was going to happen. Think of all the things you would do because Jesus was to be there! Yet when God sends a child into your home, it is as important as a visit from the Lord Himself. Why am I emphasizing this? Because it has been my observation that many people look upon children differently from this, almost wishing in some cases that they had not been born.

Verse 6 presents a contrasting truth:

> But whoso shall offend one of these little ones which believe in me, it were better for him that a millstone were hanged about his neck, and that he were drowned in the depth of the sea.

This word *offend* means "cause to stumble." Generally we use this word in regard to child evangelism. When we limit it to that, however, we are not getting the full meaning of the verse. Here is a really solemn thought. If these children whom God has sent into our homes are caused to stumble, it is better for us, hypothetically speaking, that a millstone were tied about our necks and we were cast into the sea. Let us be honest. How many of our children have been caused to stumble by those unguarded remarks we make in our homes, or by our unguarded actions—because we gave vent to our temper, because we were irritated and disturbed? How many children right in our own homes have been caused to stumble? This is an awesome thought; it should not be taken lightly. This is the position of importance that God gives children in His thoughts. Our responsibility should be considered with real concern and with real fear.

Let us look for a moment at the other side of the matter, to verify that there is another side. Although parenthood is an awesome responsibility, it can also bring great happiness and satisfaction. Look at the words of Proverbs 10:1:

A wise son maketh a glad father: but a foolish son is the heaviness of his mother.

Incidentally, notice how realistic the Word of God is on this point. When there is a wise son who is doing good things and bringing credit to the family, oh, how glad the father is. You would think that he gave birth to that son, and you would think he reared him all by himself. But do you notice what the Scripture says about a foolish son? He is the heaviness of the mother. The father is inclined to say, "He has been trained better than that. I am through with him!" It is the mother who spends time in secret with a broken heart because of a foolish son. This is an accurate passage.

But notice the first part of that statement: "A wise son maketh a glad father. . . ." I have lived long enough to have some of my children grow up. You cannot imagine the joy, the satisfaction, the thrill, and the reward there is in seeing your grown children following the course in which you have trained them.

My wife and I have prayed consistently that the Lord would give us wisdom with our children. One thing we pray earnestly for is that God will let us know when to let our children go. It is just as important to know when to let them go as it is dangerous to let them go too soon. You see, this verse on which we are basing our thoughts is true: "Train up a child according to his individual bent, and when he reaches the age of maturity he will make his decisions in line with that training." There comes a time when you have to let him go to make his own decisions. It is a real thrill to see those decisions made according to your training.

I will try to illustrate. Once when my oldest son was in college he called me and said, "Dad, I have something in mind, and I want to know if you think it is foolish or not." He told me what it was, and then he said, "I will do whatever you think." I said, "Tim, on your twenty-first birthday a few weeks ago, you wrote me a letter. You mentioned that on that birthday you had reached what we commonly think of as the 'age of responsibility.' You thanked me for everything I had done up to that time. On the basis of that, I want you to make this decision. All I am going to do is pray for you. That is all. I will pray that God will give you the wisdom and discretion to make the decision that needs to be made." I did some tall praying that night, I can assure you. A few days later I got another letter from him, and I rejoiced to see that the decision he had made was according to the way he had been trained.

All the money in the world could not have purchased the reward we had when that occurred. That was the first real test of the training about which we are thinking. Any other pleasure you might name is not equal to the pleasure of seeing this promise come true in the life of your child. You must look upon God's presentation of your children to you as a fearsome thing, because it is a great responsibility; but recognize also that there will come a day when there will be real pleasure in the reaping of the reward.

Before we leave this phase of our subject, God's sovereign right in bringing children into the world, and before we leave the matter of recognizing the value of children as God sees them, we want to try to answer some questions that probably have arisen in your minds. I trust we can do that in a way that will not be offensive to anyone, because these may be considered "delicate" matters.

The Bible teaches very plainly that the organs of sex were given to man not solely for the purpose of reproduction. They were given that the physical and emotional needs of both the man and the woman might be met. If that is not recognized, there will never be an atmosphere in the home that is healthy for the rearing of children. There are many extreme positions on this, but we want to refer to the Word of God. We will look at it without comment; we will let the Word of God speak for itself, save where a word or two might clarify a passage. First, notice a simple statement about the marriage relationship in Hebrews 13:4. It is basic; everything else stems from this:

> Marriage is honourable in all, and the bed undefiled: but whoremongers and adulterers God will judge.

Putting that very simply, it says that there is nothing dirty, there is nothing unclean, and there is nothing immoral about the marriage relationship. That needs to be emphasized, because Hollywood, novels, and religious extremists of our day have given us a completely wrong slant on marriage and sex. The Bible has the correct approach.

Think about these words in Proverbs 5:15-21:

> 15 Drink waters out of thine own cistern, and running waters out of thine own well.
> 16 Let thy fountains be dispersed abroad, and rivers of waters in the streets.
> 17 Let them be only thine own, and not strangers' with thee.
> 18 Let thy fountain be blessed: and rejoice with the wife of thy youth.
> 19 Let her be as the loving hind and pleasant roe; let her breasts satisfy thee at all times; and be thou ravished always with her love.
> 20 And why wilt thou, my son, be ravished with a strange woman, and embrace the bosom of a stranger?
> 21 For the ways of man are before the eyes of the Lord, and he pondereth all his goings.

Then notice the words of I Corinthians 7:1-5, and associate what we find here with the passage of Scripture above. The Corinthians had written to the apostle Paul because of the very trying days in which they were living, and were asking him about the matter of marriage. Because Paul himself had foregone the privileges of marriage, some people were getting the idea that he forbade marriage; they asked him about it, and this is a portion of his answer:

> 1 Now concerning the things whereof ye wrote unto me: It is good for a man not to touch a woman.

2 Nevertheless, to avoid fornication, let every man have his own wife, and let every woman have her own husband.
3 Let the husband render unto the wife due benevolence: and likewise also the wife unto the husband.
4 The wife hath not power of her own body, but the husband: and likewise also the husband hath not power of his own body, but the wife.
5 Defraud ye not one the other, except it be with consent for a time, that ye may give yourself to fasting and prayer; and come together again, that Satan tempt you not for your incontinency.

This passage concerns the marriage relationship. This is God's order. Marriage is a mutual relationship, and it was intended by God for something other than the mere reproduction of children. The reason we need to realize this is that it brings up a question that faces many young couples today. It is, "Will God send us just as many children as He wants us to have, or do we have a moral right to limit the size of our families and to space our children?"

The following opinion is purely personal. It is worth no more than any other human opinion. But in answer to such a question, I would say, first, that if a person were living in the very center of God's will, if he were walking by faith every single minute—please notice the "ifs" I am putting into this—and if conditions were continuing now as they were in the early days of creation, then a man and a woman might leave the whole matter to God. Some individuals have enough faith to do that.

Only eternity will reveal what we have missed because we did not have enough faith to walk with God as completely in this as we may have in other areas of our lives. As a concrete example, think what this world would have missed if John Wesley had never been born. What if Susanna Wesley had decided to have only three children instead of twenty-one?

Only eternity will reveal what we may have missed because we did not have enough faith to trust God and let Him do as He wished. On the other hand, I believe that the Word of God teaches that you do have a right to "space" your family if you so desire. Let me emphasize that I am not sure that this is the best thing; I am not sure that you are not missing untold blessing by doing so. But when I am asked, "Do I have a moral right, from the Word of God, to space my family?" I must answer that you do.

The Bible suggests a method of birth control, but we will not go into detail. It is significant to note that God did not give that method of birth control until the day of Moses. At that time He also gave permission for divorce. He had never given such permission before, and He said that He gave it because of the hardness of the hearts of men. I wonder if by implication we might not assume that for that same reason He gave a method of birth control—because people were not finding it as easy to walk by faith as they had in years gone by.

The method of birth control that God sanctioned is described in the writings of Moses, and it is commonly referred to today as the "rhythm method" of birth control. I do not think that God was greatly concerned about the method; I think He was concerned about the intent. You probably are aware that the rhythm method is very uncertain. The reasons for that are many. Our diets today are not right; our tensions are great; nothing works quite as well as it used to. It would be foolish to say that God does not approve of any method of birth control other than this one, just as it would be foolish to say that He does not approve of any of the advances that have been made scientifically and educationally.

What God gave to Moses in relation to medicine and sanitation was basic. Since that time, horizons have been broadened and improvements have been made. Yet we never hear anyone saying today, "No, I am not going to use those modern methods of medicine because they are not the same as those Moses had." No, we just thank God for the advancements and take advantage of them. If God's object in birth control was the intent and not the method, then conscientious Christians today have a right to use modern methods of birth control to space the births of their children.

If you choose to regulate the size of your family, there are some very definite things to keep in mind. First of all, you must not be guilty in intent of breaking the Everlasting Covenant. This covenant is described in chapter 9 of the Book of Genesis. It is a covenant that is binding on all generations to the end of time. One of the provisions of the Everlasting Covenant is the obligation of married couples to bring children into the world.

In Isaiah 24, the Everlasting Covenant is again brought to our attention. There we are told that it will be one of the issues when God judges the world at the end of time. The human race has violated the Everlasting Covenant. Any deliberate refusal on the part of a married couple to bring children into the world is a violation of the Everlasting Covenant and cannot please God!

Please keep in mind that our subject at the moment is not the spacing of children. We are talking about a deliberate, overall refusal to take advantage of the God-given opportunity of bringing children into the world.

And you must keep in mind that God has an individual will for each one of His children. This includes you and me. I believe with all my heart that God had a will in regard to the number of children that my wife and I had. I believe that had we been unresponsive to the voice of God, if we had shrugged our shoulders and said, "It doesn't matter, we are going to have only one child, or two children," we could not have known the full blessing of God upon our lives.

We sought the will of God about how many children we should have, and in the mercy of God He permitted us to have seven. That does not mean that it is God's will for everybody to have seven children. He might want you to have twenty. I do not know. What I am saying is that you as an individual Christian should not say, "I believe that on our salary we can educate two children very nicely. I believe it will be easier to raise one now and another ten years from now." (You would be wrong about that, incidentally.) You have no right to say such things, because God has a will for you.

You need, rather, to take it to the Lord in prayer, and to say, "Lord, You know us, You know our capabilities, You know what the future holds. Give us wisdom, give us understanding, direct us, and let us know how many children we should have." You have no right to plan your family simply on the basis of your selfish desires. I say this reverently: God might throw you a curve if you do.

I have had conferences through the years with couples whose hearts were heavy because their arms were empty. They have prayed to God for children, and they have asked me to pray with them. When we have gone into the subject, it has developed that they both had good jobs, they wanted to get their home paid for, and they wanted to get this nice thing and that nice thing. When they got all ready, they said, "All right, now, God, send us a child." I say this reverently also, but it is possible that in such cases God said, "I will not do it. It is not up to you to decide when your children will come without considering Me."

I believe that the barren wombs of many older married women today are due to the fact that they were selfish. They were not willing to make the sacrifices that were necessary to have children at a certain point in life.

One question very often asked in this connection is, "If God has not seen fit to give us a child, is it all right to adopt a child? Does it please the Lord, or displease Him?" Here again is a matter that must be decided on the basis of the individual and God's will for him. That is primary.

God may have withheld children from you for any number of reasons known only to Himself. Perhaps, He can use you in ways that you could not possibly be used if you had had children. There is always the possibility that God did not want you to have children because He knew the direction your life was going to take. He knew that there would be a time when you would not be able to take care of a child of your own, and knowing that, He did not send you a child. Understand, that is not always the case. There are many factors to keep in mind, but this is one possibility.

Keeping such possibilities in mind, think further of this: If children are important in the sight of God, if they are the dearest treasure with which you can be entrusted, and if God has not seen fit to give you a child, can you think of any better way to serve Him than to take some motherless child into your home and to train that child for the glory of God? If you have made a definite searching of your own heart, asking God to open the door or close the door, and God has opened the door for you to have a child that was not your own, welcome that child with your arms wide open and thank God that He has given you an opportunity to train a child for Him.

Here again is a personal opinion: I wonder if that is not one of the ways God has of making up for the mistakes that some people think He makes. Some people think, for example, that God makes a mistake in sending a child to an unwed mother. But biological laws have to be recognized. We have maintained that throughout this discussion. If men live in error, according to the flesh or in sin, and children are born to unwed mothers, perhaps God's way of evening up the situation is to permit a married woman's womb to be barren so that her heart may be big enough to take in someone else's child and make it her own. If you stop to think about it, there are not too many of us with houses full of children who would be willing to adopt some more. We have all we can manage as it is. Perhaps this is God's way of doing it.

Remember that we will never be able to understand our children unless we understand what our child means to God. From His viewpoint, that child is the most important thing in our lives and the most important thing in the world.

5

The Second Step

The first step in understanding your child is to realize the value of children in the eyes of God. The second step is no less important. In fact, it is absolutely essential. You must dedicate your child to God.

We have been basing our remarks on Proverbs 22:6, and we suggested a very literal translation of that verse. We need now to think about it again. The first word of that verse is "train." We have pointed out, and we would remind you, that the word "train" is a translation of a Hebrew word which has a variety of meanings. One of the meanings, and the one we particularly want to notice, concerns "dedication." In Deuteronomy 20 the word is used in that way. This chapter describes the activities of a young Israelite who was drafted for the armed services—some of the privileges, rights, and responsibilities that he had. As a concluding statement, verse 5 says:

> And the officers shall speak unto the people, saying, What man is there that hath built a new house, and hath not dedicated it? let him go and return to his house, lest he die in the battle, and another man dedicate it.

In this verse, notice the words "dedicate" and "dedicated." They are translations of the same Hebrew word translated "train" in Proverbs 22:6. If you are not familiar with the Hebrew and Greek in which the Scriptures were originally written, you need to be reminded that our English language is inadequate by comparison. Hebrew and Greek words have many more meanings than one. You never do fully comprehend a word unless you examine all the meanings of that particular word.

That is why we are looking at this word "train" from the standpoint of dedication. We will be looking at it from a number of standpoints later, because it does have varied meanings. But looking at it from the standpoint of dedication, you might read Proverbs 22:6 with the word "train" replaced by the word "dedicate": "Dedicate your child. . . ."

The dedication of a child is tremendously important. There is a great deal of theological discussion and disagreement as to whether or not it is actually possible to dedicate a child to the Lord. The question is whether you, an individual with an individual will, have a right to dedicate another individual, who has a will of his own, to the Lord. The argument is that you may dedicate an inanimate thing, such as a building or a chair, but you cannot dedicate an animate thing, because that animate thing has a will, and you cannot give someone else's will to God.

Although it is a subject of theological discussion, it has about as much point as the ancient theological discussion about how many angels could dance on the head of a pin. What we think is beside the point. The emphasis should be on what the Word of God says. Even though some theologians say it is impossible to dedicate a child to God, the Bible very plainly says that it was done. We cannot begin to examine all the instances where this was done, but we will look at one example.

In Proverbs 31:1-3 an instance is recorded where an individual was dedicated to the Lord, and how it came about:

1 The words of king Lemuel, the prophecy that his mother taught him,
2 What, my son? and what, the son of my womb? and what, the son of my vows?
3 Give not thy strength unto women, nor thy ways to that which destroyeth kings.

The mother of King Lemuel goes on and gives him some very practical advice that any young man needs. Lemuel is identified by some Bible scholars as King Solomon. Notice how she refers to him as "my son," "the son of my womb" and then as "the son of my vows." That word "vows" elsewhere in the Scripture is translated "dedication." It means simply "to give something to God."

People sometimes have problems in understanding the plain meaning of the English words into which the Bible is translated. All that this word "dedicate" means, basically and specifically, is "to set aside for a specific purpose" or "to declare an intention." One of the reasons why some people are afraid to talk about the dedication of children is that they assume that when you dedicate your child to the Lord you are saying that the child need not make any decision concerning his own salvation. They think you are saying that the child is saved from the moment you dedicate him to the Lord. But that is not what the word "dedicate" means, nor is it the intention of the Scripture to indicate that.

The word "dedicate" means simply that this child whom God has given to you, you give back to Him. This child whom God has given to you, you set aside by declaring your intention in regard to that child. If you dedicate your child to the Lord you are saying in so many words, "God, I want You to have him. I want You to direct his life. I want You to lead him."

Someone may say, "I do not want my son to be a preacher or a missionary; I want him to be something else. If I dedicate him to the Lord, then he will have to be a preacher or a missionary." That is not true. In the life of a Christian, there is no difference between the sacred and the secular. Everything is sacred. If you dedicate your child to the Lord and the Lord has "bent" him in the direction of medicine, you would be making a great mistake in trying to bend him in the direction of teaching or preaching or something else. When you dedicate your child to God you are simply saying, "Lord, I declare my intention. I want You to direct the life of my child."

This type of dedication is extremely important, because at the moment of dedication you put your child in a special relationship to God. Does that seem strange? In I Corinthians 7:12-14, there is an illustration of this. This passage is not talking solely about the dedication of children. It is talking about husbands, wives, and children:

> 12 But to the rest speak I, not the Lord: if any brother hath a wife that believeth not, and she be pleased to dwell with him, let him not put her away.
> 13 And the woman which hath an husband that believeth not, and if he be pleased to dwell with her, let her not leave him.
> 14 For the unbelieving husband is sanctified by the wife, and

the unbelieving wife is sanctified by the husband: else were your children unclean; but now are they holy.

These verses contain the information we need. But lest there be some misunderstanding, let us go back to verse 12 and notice the statement, "But to the rest speak I, not the Lord." Paul was not declaring that what he would be saying (in the next few verses) was not inspired. What he was saying is that the Lord had a specific commandment concerning the things which came prior to verse 12; that they were commands previously given in the Scriptures. But the Lord had not given any prior commandment in regard to the subject about which he is talking in this passage (verse 12 on). Here he is also talking by the inspiration of the Holy Spirit. He is dealing with a problem that arose in the early church, a problem that arises on mission fields today, and a problem that arises even in our society—the problem of two unbelievers, married, when one of them finds the Lord Jesus Christ as his Savior and the other does not.

Paul says that if the individual who refuses to accept Christ as his Savior is willing to stay with the believer, by all means the believer should see to it that the home is held intact. If the unbeliever wishes to depart, there is nothing the believer can do about it. That does not mean he has a right to marry somebody else; it simply means that there is no use for him to fret about it or to condemn himself for it. There is nothing he can do; he has no control over the situation. One of the reasons why Paul encourages the believing partner to stay with the unbelieving partner is that the unbelieving partner is sanctified by the relationship. Likewise, he takes the opportunity to add, the children of believing parents are sanctified by the relationship of the parents of God.

If, in thinking about the word "sanctified," you assume that it means something like a spiritual experience, so that you have the idea that the children of believing parents are automatically saved, you are misinterpreting Scripture. The last part of verse 14 says, "else were your children unclean; but now are they holy." The word "holy" and the word "sanctified" in verse 14 are both translations of the Greek word *hagias,* and mean exactly the same thing.

The word "sanctified" in its basic meaning is "set apart." What this verse of Scripture says is that the children of believing parents are set apart in the sight of God for special attention because they are near to His own children.

You are much more interested in your children than you are in my children. This is perfectly natural. When your grandchildren come along you will be much more interested in your grandchildren, because they are so closely related to your own child, than you will be in some other little baby, no matter how cute that other baby may be.

This passage of Scripture teaches that in the same way God is vitally interested in the children of believing parents. Even though the children are not saved and though they need to be saved, they are nonetheless in a special relationship to Him and secure special attention. You can understand how that would be. If you are a sincere Christian parent, you are going to be concerned about the welfare of your child and you are going to be spending some time in talking to God about your child. God cannot refuse to answer your prayer. So we would say, generally speaking at least, that the children of Christian parents have a much greater opportunity for blessing from God than do the children of non-Christian parents.

This is not because God is a respecter of persons. He is not. It is simply because Christian parents are set apart in a special relationship to God. God is interested in everything that pertains to these Christians, including their children, even if their children happen to be unsaved. We have referred to this passage of Scripture and have made these comments to show you from the Word of God that when you dedicate your child to the Lord, your child is in a special relationship to the Lord, and God has a very special interest in him—a more special interest than He would have in the child of unsaved parents.

There is a detailed illustration of this in I Samuel 1, the story of Hannah, the mother of Samuel, and of just how Samuel's birth came about. Hannah had been grieving for quite some time because she was barren, because she had no child, and she made a journey with her husband to Shiloh on the annual feast day:

> 9 So Hannah rose up after they had eaten in Shiloh, and after they had drunk. Now Eli the priest sat upon a seat by a post of the temple of the Lord.

10 And she was in bitterness of soul, and prayed unto the Lord, and wept sore.

11 And she vowed a vow, and said, O Lord of hosts, if thou wilt indeed look on the affliction of thine handmaid, and remember me, and not forget thine handmaid, but wilt give unto thine handmaid a man child, then I will give him unto the Lord all the days of his life, and there shall no razor come upon his head.

She went on praying, and God heard her prayer, and a child was born. The story continues:

20 Wherefore it came to pass, when the time was come about after Hannah had conceived, that she bare a son, and called his name Samuel, saying, Because I have asked him of the Lord.

(The word "Samuel" is a transliteration of the Hebrew word *shemoel,* which actually means "ask of the Lord.")

21 And the man Elkanah, and all his house, went up to offer unto the Lord the yearly sacrifice, and his vow.

22 But Hannah went not up; for she said unto her husband, I will not go up until the child be weaned, and then I will bring him, that he may appear before the Lord, and there abide forever.

23 And Elkanah her husband said unto her, Do what seemeth thee good; tarry until thou have weaned him; only the Lord establish his word. So the woman abode, and gave her son suck until she weaned him.

24 And when she had weaned him, she took him up with her, with three bullocks, and one ephah of flour, and a bottle of wine, and brought him unto the house of the Lord in Shiloh: and the child was young.

25 And they slew a bullock, and brought the child to Eli.

26 And she said, O my lord, as thy soul liveth, my lord, I am the woman that stood by thee here, praying unto the Lord.

27 For this child I prayed; and the Lord hath given me my petition which I asked of him:

28 Therefore also I have lent him to the Lord; as long as he liveth he shall be lent to the Lord. And he worshipped the Lord there.

Notice the word "lent" in verse 28 and the word "asked" in verse 27. These two words are translations of the same root in Hebrew as the word "Samuel." The root word is *shawal.* It is a play on words, so to speak; Hannah is saying, "I shawaled this child from You, and now I shawal him back to You." That is the meaning of the word translated "lent." Hannah dedicated her child to God.

It has already been pointed out, whether you believe it or not, that, if you have a child, God permitted you to have that child. God gave him to you. It was not something that just happened—not just a biological accident. God permitted you to have that child.

Since He did, and since the child is that important to God, then you have a real obligation to give him back to God, to dedicate him to the Lord. What does that mean? Does it mean that you have a little public service where you go down to the front of the church and the minister reads a dedication service, and then you go on your way, saying, "I have dedicated my child to the Lord"? There is nothing wrong with a public dedication service; as a matter of fact, when the Lord leads it, it can be an impressive and effective experience.

But your responsibility does not end with that public dedication service, nor does it end with a private dedication service. The moment we knew that each one of our seven children was conceived, we knelt beside our bed, a place where we have talked to God often and long about our children. We bowed on our knees by that bed and dedicated that child to the Lord. We never have had a public dedication service for our children. We did not wait until after they were born. The moment we knew they were conceived, we dedicated them to the Lord.

We did not get up off our knees and wash our hands of the whole thing, saying, "Now we have dedicated our child to the Lord; everything is going to be just fine." Instead, we renewed our vows to the Lord for all our children, while recognizing the responsibility that was ours in relation to the new child. That is exactly what Hannah did. For example, in the story in I Samuel, when Hannah had given birth to this child and Elkanah her husband said, "Come and go with me on this trip to Shiloh," she said, "No, my responsibility is here at home with my son."

This trip to Shiloh that they had been making every year was mandatory for the men. The women did not have to go as a religious responsibility. She went along to keep her husband company. She had gone before, and he thought she would go again. But she said, "No, I am not going with you any more until Samuel is weaned."

This should not be taken to mean that young mothers should never go on trips with their husbands. Nor is it suggesting that they should never leave their children alone. It does suggest, however, that if there is ever a question in your mind about the welfare of your children in view of a trip that you have in mind, your place is at home. This is part of the dedication—taking full responsibility for the welfare of the children. This matter of dedicating a child is not just a matter of saying, "Lord, I give You my child; take care of him now." Rather, you dedicate your child to the Lord, and in so doing, you accept the responsibility that is involved in that dedication.

This matter of the weaning of Samuel is very interesting. I do not know how we could arrive at a dogmatic decision about it. Hannah may have been talking about the weaning of Samuel from her breast. If she was, Samuel was three years old when he was weaned, and she stayed at home with him for those three years. She said to her husband, "He needs me; you do not. You go on and make the trip without me."

There was another weaning of children, however, that was recognized in Judaism—a weaning at the age of ten, when the children were weaned from the ordinary cares and instructions of the home and placed under the care of tutors and scholars. I do not know how we can be sure which of these weanings is indicated here. Since we read that Samuel was taken to the temple and left there and that his mother did not see him again except once a year when she took him a new coat, I would be inclined to think the age was ten instead of three. Regardless of what the age was, the point is that even though Hannah lent him to the Lord, she did not shirk her responsibility while he was at home, nor did she shirk her responsibility after he began his activity in the temple.

That becomes very evident when we examine the word translated "lent" from the standpoint of its etymological meaning. The best way to do that is to look at I Chronicles 4:10. We are interested in only one word in verse 10, but we will include verse 9 to get the sense of the passage:

9 And Jabez was more honourable than his brethren: and his

mother called his name Jabez, saying, Because I bare him with sorrow.

10 And Jabez called on the God of Israel, saying, Oh, that thou wouldest bless me indeed, and enlarge my coast, and that thine hand might be with me, and that thou wouldest keep me from evil, that it may not grieve me! And God granted him that which he requested.

Notice in verse 10 the word "requested." It is a translation of the Hebrew word *shawal,* which is translated "lent" in the story about Hannah and her son Samuel.

Therefore when we talk about lending a child to the Lord, we are not talking about a dedication service that causes us to go off and say, "Well, everything is all right; I gave my child to the Lord." We are talking about the assumption of the responsibility that is closely related to a prayer life. Just as certainly as you must recognize that your child is important to God if you are to understand his individual bent, so must you recognize that if you are to train that child accordingly, you will have to spend a lot of time on your knees requesting.

This word also means "request of the Lord." Hannah made a request of the Lord concerning her son Samuel when he was dedicated to the Lord. I am a literalist when it comes to the interpretation of the Word of God. When anything is symbolic it should be recognized as symbolic; when it is literal we should not try to spiritualize it. I believe that this passage of Scripture teaches that we as Christian parents have the privilege—indeed, the responsibility—to request things from the Lord for our children.

Because God in His grace has given my wife and me children that range in age over a period of fourteen years, we pretty well have run the gamut of all the experiences any parent could possibly have with children. We had no hesitancy at all in making requests of the Lord for our children. We request help for them, and we request favor in the sight of men for them.

For example, popularity is probably tremendously important to your child. If he comes home from school and indicates that he is not as well received among the people at school as he might be, what do you do about it? Do you say, "Oh, well, forget it. It does not matter." Or do you argue with the teacher because she is not training your child properly? Or do you call the parents of some of the other children on the telephone and say, "Why don't you train your little brat to act as he ought so my kid would not have such a hard time?" What do you do about it?

Well, there are a number of things you can do. You can talk to your own child and remind him that "he who would have friends must show himself friendly." There are a lot of practical things that you can say. But after you have said them all, you can get on your knees and request that God give your child favor in the sight of his associates. And He will. But I am not suggesting that you give the child no other training. We will be talking about other kinds of training a little farther on. We are not suggesting that you should pamper your child and make a spoiled brat out of him until nobody likes him, and then say, "Lord, let people love him." But the point is that when you have trained your child in the way you should train him, you should not neglect this business of making requests of the Lord for him.

When our oldest son was in high school, he wanted to be president of the student body. He had a testimony for the Lord; there were a lot of things he would not do because his Christian convictions would not permit him to do them. But he did not go around with a sign on his back saying, "I am a Christian, and I do not do this and I do not do that." As a matter of fact, he bent over backwards to keep from being thought "pious," as he called it.

He came to me one day in my study and said, "Dad, do you think it would be feasible for me to run for president of the student body?" I said, "Why? Do you want to do it?" He said, "I would like to have the job. It is an experience I would like to have." I said, "For what other reason do you want the office?" He said, "Well, I feel sorry for the Christian kids. A lot of the Christian kids have nothing to do at the end of the school year. Most of the kids in leadership want some kind of program that Christian kids do not feel they can enter into. Of course, they always provide something for the Christian kids, but it is always sort of a second-class thing. I would like to do something about that if I could."

I said, "If I were you, and if I felt that I had even half a chance, I would run for the office." He did run for the office, and night after night all during the campaign our house was full of kids on his campaign staff, making posters and all the rest of it; he worked hard for that office—real hard.

On election day he asked us to come and hear the campaign speech that he was to give before the student body. Some of the opposition were so bent on his not getting that office that they had their men posted at the back of the auditorium to let loose a whole sack of marbles just as he began to speak, and they rolled down the floor of the auditorium into the orchestra pit. He just waited until it was all over, and then he made a speech that lasted about two minutes—the simplest speech a person could possibly make.

The entire student body, faculty and all, stood on their feet and gave him one of the few standing ovations that had been given in that school. I do not think they gave him that standing ovation because of the speech he made; it was so simple. I do not really think they gave him that ovation because of the boy he is, because he is not a particularly outstanding or unusual personality. I think they gave him the ovation because his mother and I, on our knees by our bed, requested God to give him that office, if it could bring glory to His name. And God did.

I am being very practical. I believe that we have a right as Christian parents, if we have dedicated our children to the Lord, to request things from God for them.

In I Samuel 22:9-10 there is another illustration of this word sometimes translated "dedication." It is the story about how David, before he became king, fled for his life from Saul and went to one of the priests, Ahimelech, to ask for help. Doeg, an Edomite spy, made a report to Saul about it:

> 9 Then answered Doeg the Edomite, which was set over the servants of Saul, and said, I saw the son of Jesse coming to Nob, to Ahimelech the son of Ahitub.
> 10 And he enquired of the Lord for him, and gave him victuals, and gave him the sword of Goliath the Philistine.

According to the custom of the day, David, because he did not know which way to turn, went to the priest and said, "Will you talk to God about me? Will you enquire of the Lord?" This word "enquired" in verse 10 is a translation of the Hebrew word *shawal*.

When we talk about lending our child to the Lord, about dedicating our child to the Lord, we are not talking about just turning the child over to the Lord and forgetting him. We are saying to the

Lord, "Lord, here he is. This gives us a right to demand Your special interest in him." You as parents have a right to inquire of the Lord concerning your child. You have a right to ask the Lord for direction and wisdom in deciding what to do.

Your child will come to you some day with questions for which you do not have the answers. It will not do for you to say, "Oh, I don't know; forget it." And it will not do for you to say, "I will talk to you about that another time," unless you say that just to get a little time with the Lord.

Sometimes my children have come to me with questions for which I did not have the answer, and I have said, "How about our talking about that tomorrow when we will have more time?" Well, technically we did need more time, but it was not so much that we needed more time to talk together about it as that I needed more time to inquire of the Lord. I believe that by faith you can inquire of the Lord; you can say, "Lord, what should I do in this particular instance?" and the Lord will let you know what you should do.

I do not believe in visions and voices; I do not believe that the Lord will come down and tap you on the shoulder or that you will turn around and see a great big light and then say, "The Lord spoke to me." But the Lord can so arrange circumstances that when you have inquired of the Lord in this fashion, you will have the right answer to give at the right time.

Judges 18 tells the story of the nation of Israel when the priesthood had neglected their duty and the priests were few and far between. One day some travelers came across a priest who was living in the home of a man who wanted to worship God. The priest was in his employ as a sort of private chaplain. When these strangers found this priest:

> 5 . . . they said unto him, Ask counsel, we pray thee, of God, that we may know whether our way which we go shall be prosperous.

In other words, they were saying: "We are headed out in a certain direction. You ask God whether it is going to be a prosperous way or not. Ask counsel." The words "Ask counsel" are a translation of this one Hebrew word *shawal* about which we are talking, and this suggests another idea about dedication.

We are talking about the right you have as a Christian parent to ask of the Lord counsel for directing your child—to ask His advice. We have counselors today in our public schools, and I am grateful for all the good they are able to do. But with all due respect to them, before I would turn my child over to a counselor in a public school, I would ask counsel of the Lord for him. I would find out what God thinks about it, because much of the human counsel that is available today is not based upon the principles of Scripture. It is based upon the principles of men.

Such advice is often more misleading than helpful. I do not mean to be critical when I say that; I am talking about the responsibility of Christian parents. It is not your responsibility to turn your child over to a counselor on a school payroll. It is your responsibility as a parent to seek counsel of the Lord. The Lord may direct you to that counselor, or He may direct you to another counselor, or He may bring you into contact with some of your neighbors or friends who have had exactly the same problem and who have learned the correct approach by trial and error or by experience. You can learn from that. But you first should exercise your right to ask counsel of the Lord.

Another incident in which a couple dedicated their child to the Lord in a practical fashion is found in Judges 13. When you have the time, read the whole chapter. Here is the story of a man, by the name of Manoah, and his wife. They were childless, and their empty arms hungered for a child. They had prayed much for a child. One day, according to verse 3,

> . . . the angel of the Lord appeared unto the woman, and said unto her, Behold now, thou art barren, and bearest not: but thou shalt conceive, and bear a son.

This phrase, "the angel of the Lord," in the Old Testament (you can verify this when you have the time to study it for yourself) is the title for the Lord Jesus Christ of the New Testament.

The first time the Lord Jesus Christ came to earth was not when He came as a babe in Bethlehem's manger; the Lord Jesus Christ had been on earth many times prior to that. This is one of those times. He came and said to this godly woman whose arms yearned for a child, "You shall have a child." She went home and told her husband about it. He was both thrilled and frightened, because he knew that God had spoken. His response is recorded in verse 8:

> Then Manoah intreated the Lord, and said, O my Lord, let the man of God which thou didst send come again unto us, and teach us what we shall do unto the child that shall be born.

Did you notice when they began praying for this child? They began when he was conceived, before he was born. They did not begin praying for their child after he got into some trouble. Before he was ever born, they said, "Lord, tell us how to train this child according to the way that Thou wouldst have him brought up." (I wonder what would happen if all Christian parents, every time they knew that a child was conceived, would get on their knees and ask God to give them wisdom about how to train that child. I wonder if that would not solve our juvenile delinquency problem. I wonder if it would not spare parents some of the problems they face as their children get along in life.)

> 12 And Manoah said, Now let thy words come to pass. How shall we order the child, and how shall we do unto him?

It is interesting to notice that the Angel of the Lord answered Manoah with instructions about the prenatal activity of his wife:

> 13 And the angel of the Lord said unto Manoah, Of all that I said unto the woman let her beware.
> 14 She may not eat of any thing that cometh of the vine, neither let her drink wine or strong drink, nor eat any unclean thing: all that I commanded her let her observe.

Each of these things had a special relationship to the Hebrew economy. We would not suggest that they would be any more enforceable upon mothers today than the commandment not to eat pork. What we are saying, however, is that there is a principle involved. God said that one of the best ways to train your child is for the mother to take care of herself during pregnancy.

Only a very thorough study of case histories, which would be almost impossible because conditions cannot be controlled, would prove fully the differences there might be in children if mothers had properly cared for themselves before their children were born. But there is enough evidence available to show that many children are born with emotional problems because of improper care by the mother before the birth of the child.

Do you see what we are emphasizing? When we speak of dedicating a child to the Lord, we do not have in mind a religious service in which you stand up in front of a congregation with a little baby in your arms and go through some kind of vow-taking. What we are saying is that you and your husband, together on your knees before the Lord, should dedicate your child to the Lord. As you dedicate your child to the Lord, recognize the responsibility of prayer for the child on your part as a parent before the Lord. Recognize not only the responsibility, but the privilege of making requests of the Lord for your child. Do not be afraid to ask for things for your child. God is more interested in your child than you may think. Do not ever hesitate to ask counsel of the Lord in regard to your child. Do not hesitate to inquire of the Lord for your child. Keep in mind that this will work only if you are vitally interested in its working.

Let me give you one verse, Psalm 27:4, that will emphasize that:

> One thing have I desired of the Lord, that will I seek after; that I may dwell in the house of the Lord all the days of my life, to behold the beauty of the Lord, and to enquire in his temple.

Look at the word "desired." It is a translation of the word *shawal* at which we have been looking, the same word translated "train" and translated "dedicate." What does it mean? It means that when you dedicate your child to the Lord, you have a deep desire in your heart to see accomplished in his heart and life that which is best.

Again it should be emphasized that when we speak of dedication, we do not mean what is commonly referred to as "full-time Christian service." That is a decision that your child will have to make for himself.

There are in the ministry today a great many ministers who are miserable for the reason that they are not there because they think that God wants them there. They are there because they did not want to disappoint their mothers. Their mothers told them that they gave them to God to be preachers, and they did not want to disappoint their mothers. You do not have any right to give your child to God to be a preacher. All you need do is to give him to God.

Permit one final illustration. I have five daughters. From the time she was old enough to lisp, the oldest one has wanted to be in love. We had very definite rules, incidentally, about the way she dated, whom she dated, when she dated, and how she dated, but she was popular. She never did go with one boy very long, because she wanted to be in love—and I am not referring simply to the physical aspects of love.

My wife and I discussed it one day, and then we discussed it with her. I said, "You want to be in love. You have gone with a lot of boys, but you turn up your nose at them and say, 'That is not what I want.' What is it you want? What is it you are looking for that you call love?" Her eyes filled with tears and she got real quiet, and she said, "Well, Daddy, I will tell you. I want to fall in love with somebody who will make a relationship for me like the one you and Mother have. I want to be in love as you and Mother are in love. I want somebody to be like you, and I want to be like Mother for somebody. That is what I am looking for in love."

My wife and I got on our knees, and we made a request of the Lord. You may think the Lord is not interested in a thing like this, but I believe He is. We said, "Lord, send somebody into her life. Send into her life some boy who will meet those needs."

The story of how God answered that prayer is too long to go into here, but in a most unusual way, God answered that prayer. I do not expect ever to have any in-law problems because I am not afraid to request of the Lord a very practical thing like a love affair for my child.

That is what it means when you dedicate your child to the Lord; you are not afraid to ask God for the thing that you deeply desire for the child. If you love your children, even though they may not realize it sometimes, your heart aches when their hearts ache, and your heart rejoices when theirs rejoice.

6

Hindrances to Prayer

As we realize the tremendous importance of praying for the everyday needs of our children, there are two points to keep in mind. The first is that only those who have accepted Christ as Savior have the privilege to pray in this manner. The only prayer that an unsaved person can make with any expectation of being heard is, "God be merciful to me a sinner" (Luke 18:13), or words to that effect.

But after we have said that, we should recognize also that many who have accepted Christ as Savior pray but feel that their prayers are not effective at all, or at least not as effective as they would like for them to be. Their prayers are "hindered." There are many reasons why prayers are hindered, and that would be a discussion in itself. But one of the reasons given in Scripture for the hindrance of prayer is directly related to the subject which we have been discussing. The suggestion is made in I Peter 3:1-7:

> 1 Likewise, ye wives, be in subjection to your own husbands; that, if any obey not the word, they also may without the word be won by the conversation of the wives;
>
> 2 While they behold your chaste conversation coupled with fear.
>
> 3 Whose adorning let it not be that outward adorning of plaiting the hair, and of wearing of gold, or of putting on of apparel,
>
> 4 But let it be the hidden man of the heart, in that which is not corruptible, even the ornament of a meek and quiet spirit, which is in the sight of God of great price.
>
> 5 For after this manner in the old time the holy women also, who trusted in God, adorned themselves, being in subjection unto their own husbands:

6 Even as Sara obeyed Abraham, calling him lord: whose daughters ye are, as long as ye do well, and are not afraid with any amazement.

7 Likewise, ye husbands, dwell with them according to knowledge, giving honour unto the wife, as unto the weaker vessel, and as being heirs together of the grace of life; that your prayers be not hindered.

Notice particularly the phrase in verse 7 that says, "that your prayers be not hindered."

The subject of this entire passage in I Peter is family relationships. It would follow, therefore, that the prayers mentioned in verse 7 are family prayers, or more specifically, prayers of the husband and wife for the family. Here it is stated that it is definitely possible for the prayers of a husband and wife to be hindered.

Since we are talking about the family, and of course there is nothing of any greater importance in the family than the children, let us center our thinking upon the suggestion that the prayers of a mother and a father for their children can be hindered.

Although there are many reasons for prayers being hindered, this passage of Scripture, besides pointing out that it is possible, also gives a basic reason for such hindrances: The relationship that exists between the husband and wife regulates the manner in which God answers prayer. In other words, the relationship between the husband and wife either helps or hinders the manner in which God answers.

The word "hinder" may bring several pictures to our mind, because the English word has several meanings. But think particularly about the meaning of the Greek word that is translated by our English word "hinder," since Greek is the language in which Peter wrote. It is the Greek word *enkopto,* which literally means "to cut into." Back of many Greek words are pictures. Most of these pictures are suggested by their use in classical Greek, and they sometimes help us to understand the meaning of the word. The picture back of this particular word is that of a man trying to impede the progress of a group of people who are coming in his direction. There does not seem to be any other way to stop their onrush, so he runs up the road toward them so they cannot move with the ease they would ordinarily.

So this word literally means "to cut into" something, with the motive of hindering its effectiveness. In just that way Satan can hinder our prayers, can cut into them, and make them less effective than they would otherwise be. One way he can do that is by leading husbands and wives into the wrong relationship, thus making their prayers ineffective.

In Acts 24 this word is used in a somewhat different manner. Perhaps the way the word is used in this chapter, which is the record of the testimony of the apostle Paul before the Roman governor Felix, is characteristic of your praying. In addressing Felix, Paul said:

> 4 Notwithstanding, that I be not further tedious unto thee, I pray thee that thou wouldest hear us of thy clemency a few words.

Notice the word "tedious"; it is a translation of our word *enkopto*. This verse suggests, then, that the relationship of a husband and wife can be such that even their praying together can become tedious.

If it were possible to make a survey of how many believing husbands and wives exercise this tremendous privilege of praying together, we would probably be surprised, even alarmed, at the results. Of those few who do exercise this privilege it would be interesting also to know for how many prayer is a time of joy, blessing, and effectiveness, and for how many it has become a tedious time. Unfortunately, many would have to say, "Frankly, it became so tedious that we have almost stopped praying altogether."

The passage in I Peter 3 implies that it is possible for the relationship of the husband and wife to become such that their prayers are hindered because of the tedium of the situation.

In chapter 4 of the Gospel of John, this word *enkopto* is used in still another way. This usage, too, can give us an idea of the ways in which our prayers can be hindered. This passage gives the record of the Lord Jesus Christ sitting on the curb of Jacob's well and dealing with the Samaritan woman:

> 6 Now Jacob's well was there. Jesus therefore, being wearied with his journey, sat thus on the well: and it was about the sixth hour.

The word "wearied" in this verse is another translation of the word that is translated "hindered" in I Peter and "tedious" in Acts. The relationship of the husband and wife, then, can become such that their prayers will be hindered; they will become tedious to them and they will become wearied with them.

Incidentally, our actions as parents have a tremendous effect upon our children. I wonder whether we realize how quickly our children recognize our insincerity in prayer? I wonder whether we realize how quickly our children notice that some of our prayers are just words, a mere ritual? I had that forcibly brought to my attention once when we had some guests for dinner. I said grace, as I usually do, and when I had finished one of my children said, "Daddy, why did you pray that way? Because we have company?" I said, "What do you mean?" and he said, "Well, usually it is just a short prayer, but today you must be showing off, because you said so many things." That was not very flattering to me, but it serves to illustrate the point.

I mention this to emphasize that if our praying can become wearisome to us, what can it be to our children? Perhaps that is one of the reasons why some children just tolerate family devotions rather than enjoying them. Perhaps that is one reason why they want to get away just as soon as they can.

The basic idea is that it is possible for the prayer life to be hindered when the relationship between husband and wife is not what it should be. Such a possibility is of particular interest when we remember the importance of prayer in child training, to say nothing of the other areas of life.

Let us go back to I Peter 3 and see what the Spirit of God has to say about the responsibilities of the husband and wife in the marriage relationship. This passage of seven verses is one of the basic passages of Scripture dealing with the marriage relationship. If you will look at the passage, you will notice a very interesting and significant thing. Six of the verses deal with the obligations of the wife, and one verse deals with the obligations of the husband.

That seems terribly out of proportion and terribly unfair. But if there must be a reason for it, it would seem to be that the obligation of the woman, although not necessarily greater, is harder to fulfill than that of the man, and therefore God has more to say about it.

This chapter begins with the word "Likewise," which refers

back to I Peter 2:18, of the preceding chapter:

> Servants, be subject to your masters with all fear; not only to the good and gentle, but also to the froward.

In this verse, a discussion of subjection is begun. First mentioned among those who are to be in subjection are servants. This group is addressed through verse 25, the end of the chapter. Notice that the servants are told that although some masters may be good and gentle, others may be "froward"—that is, unreasonable, unlovely, and hard to get along with.

In chapter 3, in the same vein, the Holy Spirit says:

> 1 Likewise, ye wives, be in subjection to your own husbands; that, if any obey not the word, they also may without the word be won by the conversation of the wives.

Very often in discussing the principles set forth in this passage, someone will say, "Suppose my husband is not a Christian. Am I still under this obligation?" or, "Suppose my wife is not a believer? Does this still apply to me?"

This passage of Scripture implies that in this instance the husband is unsaved. Not only is he unsaved, but he is unreasonable, he is implacable, and he is a regular beast. Yet this passage also says, "Wives, be in subjection to your own husbands"—to even that kind of a husband. That should be made just as forceful as possible, else the full impact of the Scripture will be missed.

The reason for this seemingly harsh demand is given in the last part of verse 1: ". . . that, if any obey not the word. . . ." In the original text this verse contains a word that can be translated "even"; the idea is that even if they do not obey the Word of God, even if they are rebellious against the Word of God, they also may be won by the conversation of their wives. The word "conversation" here does not mean "talk"; it means "manner of life." They may be won by the manner of life of their wives.

It says "without the word." In the original text the article "the" is not found before "word," so it is not a reference to the Word of God. It is a reference, rather, to the fact that the husband may be won without the wife's saying anything at all—won because she is taking the place that God intended her to take, as outlined in the Scripture.

Usually when these thoughts are presented, some woman will

come along and say, "But you don't know my husband." No, but God does. And furthermore, He knew him when He wrote these words, and He makes no exception. Wives are to be in subjection to their husbands, and if they are in subjection to their husbands, they have a promise from God: God will deal with their husbands. God will bring their husbands around to the proper place.

It may be that God's plan seems impossible to you, but have you ever tried it? Think for a moment about this word "subjection," because it is a source of worry to some. For example, many people delete the word "obey" from the marriage ceremony, which indicates how they feel about this matter of subjection.

This word may be considered from the standpoint of grammatical construction. Such a consideration reveals that the decision as to whether or not to be in subjection is entirely the responsibility of the wife.

There is a tremendous difference between subjection that is forced and subjection that is chosen. This verse literally says, "Likewise, ye wives, submit your own selves to your own husbands." Incidentally, the grammatical construction also indicates that this is to be a continual thing. It is not a matter of submitting to the husband during the engagement period or during the marriage ceremony and then taking things over later. It is a continual manner of life, and the decision is to be made by the wife.

The word translated "subjection" or "submission" —"submit," if you prefer—is not the word ordinarily used in Scripture for the word "subjection." Rather, it is the Greek word *hupotasso*. This is a military term, and the meaning it conveys is that of "taking your place according to rank." It means only that. It does not suggest becoming a slave who has no will of her own. It simply means that you recognize that there is a place God has specified for you, and you willingly take that place.

How effective would an army be if the sergeant suddenly decided that he was going to be the general? Or if a private decided that he was going to be the commander-in-chief? The only efficient organization is one in which every member of the organization takes his proper place. The husband and wife, father and mother, are two instruments in God's hands for a specific purpose. They, too, work best when they work together, each in his proper place.

Chapter 11 of I Corinthians is one passage of Scripture that tells what the proper places are. This chapter deals with a number of corrections that needed to be made in the church at Corinth. Most of the Christians living at Corinth had been saved out of heathenism. Unfortunately, they had brought over into Christianity some of their heathen practices. One misunderstanding had to do with the relationship between the man and the woman in marriage.

In heathendom, women were mere chattels; they had no rights of their own and therefore no will of their own. They were mistreated in ways too horrible to describe here. When they became Christians and the wonderful liberty of the grace of God was proclaimed, many of these women, as well as the men, misconstrued the teaching, and the marriage relationship was in jeopardy. So the apostle Paul wrote to correct that situation, and in so doing established the principles that are stated in I Corinthians 11:3.

> But I would have you know, that the head of every man is Christ; and the head of the woman is the man; and the head of Christ is God.

This is an eternal principle. It is not limited to any one generation or to any one city. The head of every man is Christ, the head of Christ is God, and the head of the woman is the man. As a matter of fact, this very principle is explained by a statement written in the Word of God many years before this verse was written. In Genesis 2:18 we read:

> And the Lord God said, It is not good that the man should be alone; I will make him an help meet for him.

That is exactly what He did. The woman is the complement of the man. A man without a woman is like a triangle without the final line. It is not complete and never will be. If a man tries to carry on a home, ignoring the place that the woman was given by God, trouble results.

This matter of submitting oneself to one's husband is not a matter of giving up all rights and becoming nothing more than a robot. It is a matter of willingly taking the place that God, in His wisdom and in His providence, assigned: God, the head of Christ; Christ, the head of the man; and man, the head of the woman.

In Ephesians 5:22-24 there is a statement that explains how a woman can take this appointed place:

22 Wives, submit yourselves unto your own husbands, as unto the Lord.
23 For the husband is the head of the wife, even as Christ is the head of the church: and he is the saviour of the body.
24 Therefore as the church is subject unto Christ, so let the wives be to their own husbands in every thing.

A careful examination of verse 22 will reveal that it does not say that a wife is to look to her husband in the place of God. What the verse suggests, rather, is that as a wife submits herself to the Lord, she will find it easy to take the place that God ordained for her in relation to her husband.

Another truth revealed in this passage is to be found in verse 24. Notice the phrase "so let the wives be to their own husbands in every thing." Sometimes wives have been known to say, "I think it is all right to be subject to my husband, but there are a lot of things that my husband does not know anything about, and I just take those things on myself whether he likes it or not." You can take that attitude if you like—divorce rates increase every year. But that is not what God says. God says, "Wives, submit yourselves, subject yourselves, take your place as a wife in relation to your husband in everything."

Let us think again about the first seven verses of I Peter 3, because in them are suggested three things that characterize the woman who is taking the place that God intended her to have. The first of these is found in verse 2. There you will notice a reference to a "chaste conversation." That English phrase does not really convey what the Holy Spirit had in mind as He wrote through the hand of Peter. It is made more understandable when we realize that when the King James Version was translated, the word "conversation" indicated that you could tell what a person was by what he said. Unfortunately, that day is past. The phrase "manner of life" is much more expressive of the actual thought in the language of today.

What is this "chaste manner of life" of which the apostle speaks? We might more easily understand it if we realize that the word "chaste" is an unhappy translation also. Ordinarily when we think of a chaste individual, we think of someone who is sexually pure or a person who is very modest. But all of those things could be true of an individual and still not touch the subject that Peter had in mind. This word is a translation of a Greek word that means "to be without fault," and it is used in a very limited sense. Actually, it is used almost without exception to indicate being without fault in connection with the subject being discussed. The idea is not so much that wives are to be without fault as that they should be without fault in being in subjection to their husbands.

If you wonder why things have not been going well in your home or if you wonder why God does not seem to be answering your prayers for your children as you would like Him to, do you suppose it could be because you are at fault in this particular thing? Women who are taking the place that God intended they should take will manifest a "chaste conversation" in the true sense of the word.

If you will look at the last part of I Peter 3:2 you will find the phrase "coupled with fear." This suggests the second characteristic of the woman who is in subjection. Not only does she have a chaste manner of life, but that manner of life is coupled with fear, according to this verse. Most women begin to bristle when that word comes into the conversation. Some women say, "I have not seen a man yet that I was afraid of. My husband need not think he can scare me to death. I can do just as much as he can."

Recently I had a conference with a woman who told me that her husband maltreated her by kicking her as she passed him, and I said, "What did you do about it?" She replied, "I went to the closet and got a baseball bat. I'm not afraid of him. I can dish it out as well as he can." Well, that may be a humorous touch, but that is not the attitude that Peter recommends here.

Peter's word translated "fear" does not refer to the type of fear that causes a woman to do something because she is afraid of what might happen if she does not. Ephesians 5:33 says:

> Nevertheless let every one of you in particular so love his wife even as himself; and the wife see that she reverence her husband.

The word "reverence" in this verse is a translation of the same Greek word that is translated "fear" in I Peter 3. A woman who takes her God-given place in the marriage relationship will strive to maintain it without fault. She will reverence her husband.

Sometimes we may not understand our Bibles because we do not know the Greek and Hebrew languages, and certainly it is an asset to know them. But one of the reasons we do not understand our Bibles a great many times is simply that we are not familiar with the English language and all that it expresses.

The Amplified Version of the New Testament is a translation in which the editors have attempted to make the Word of God more meaningful by giving all the meanings of the English word, and as many of the synonyms for that word as are needed. It usually makes the meaning much clearer. I Peter 3:2 in that version says:

> When they observe the pure and modest way in which you conduct yourselves, together with your reverence [for your husband. That is, you are to feel for him all that reverence includes]—to respect, defer to, revere him; [revere means] to esteem, honor, [appreciate, prize] and [in the human sense] adore him; [and adore means] to admire, praise, be devoted to, deeply love, and enjoy [your husband].

It should be clear that the word "fear" means more than just running and hiding in the closet when the husband comes home at night. The idea, rather, is subjection. It involves reverence on the part of the wife for the husband, and it implies that the wife will do all she can to be faultless in this regard.

Here is an application. If you as a mother have little or no respect for your husband, don't you think it will be difficult for the children to have respect for him? Even though you may say that you do respect him, your actions may indicate otherwise. Consider, for example, what would happen in your household if the father makes a certain rule for the children; then, as fathers so often do (as it is so easy to do), he goes off to work and leaves you to enforce the rule. If you fail to enforce it, you leave the child with the impression that you think, "It doesn't really matter. You do not really have to respect Daddy's word, because I don't respect it. If I respected it, I would see to it that you did the thing that he said for you to do." This is exactly what is involved in reverence for your husband.

First Peter 3 not only suggests that the wife should be faultless in subjection to her husband and that she should respect him, but it also suggests a third characteristic of the wife who is in her proper place:

> 3 Whose adorning let it not be that outward adorning of

plaiting the hair, and of wearing of gold, or of putting on of
apparel;
4 But let it be the hidden man of the heart, in that which is not
corruptible, even the ornament of a meek and quiet spirit,
which is in the sight of God of great price.

These verses suggest that the woman who is taking her proper
place will be both spiritually and physically attractive. Peter recognizes a factor in the lives of women that is significant even
today—that it is hard to strike a happy medium. Some women are
so interested in being physically attractive that all their time is
spent on their adorning. Some feel that verse 3 forbids all plaiting
of the hair and wearing of gold. If this be the case, however, we
must also concede that it also forbids the wearing of clothes! On
the contrary, the verse suggests that time should be spent on this
aspect of life.

This is extremely important. In the counseling I have done
through the years, I have discovered many problems that can be
traced to this very thing. Sometimes women are so busy providing
a good home for their husbands and children that they are careless
about the way they look.

I Corinthians 11:7 says that the woman is the glory of the man.
God has so ordained it that the man wants to be proud of the
woman he has married; he does not want to have to make an
apology for her. Do not be afraid to spend some time on physical
adorning. Do not even be afraid to spend some of your husband's
money along this line; it is impossible to adorn yourself effectively
unless you do. Sometimes women think they are doing their husbands a favor by saving his money, when actually they could
accomplish more by spending some of it in this way.

Verse 4 presents the other side of the coin. There the suggestion
is made that the adorning should not be all outward. There should
be an inward adorning as well. If a choice between the two has to
be made, a woman would do better to choose the latter, because it
is amazing what a lovely personality can cover up.

Perhaps you have had the experience of being in the presence of
a woman who was immaculately attired, but after only a few
minutes you realized that hers was entirely an outward adorning.
She was attractive outwardly but not inwardly.

On the other hand, it is interesting to notice the women whose husbands never look at another woman, even though the wives may not be adorned as attractively as other women. But they have spent time in adorning themselves inwardly. They have a spirit and a personality that are attractive.

As a conclusion to his discussion of the wife's responsibility, Peter cites an example in verses 5 and 6:

> 5 For after this manner in the old time the holy women also, who trusted in God, adorned themselves, being in subjection unto their own husbands:
> 6 Even as Sarah obeyed Abraham, calling him lord: whose daughters ye are, as long as ye do well, and are not afraid with any amazement.

What is the conclusion that Peter draws? Look at the phrase "not afraid with any amazement." Literally that means "Do not let anything frighten you, or deter you, from this course." He uses Sarah from the Old Testament as an example.

The Amplified Version of the New Testament clarifies the application of this phrase:

> It was thus that Sarah obeyed Abraham [following his guidance and acknowledging his headship over her by] calling him lord—master, leader, authority. And you are now her true daughters if you do right and let nothing terrify you—not giving way to hysterical fears or letting anxieties unnerve you.

There are many women today who, because of anxiety, have stepped out of the place that God ordained for them. Fear and worry that the husband would not be able to accomplish enough has caused them to "take over," so to speak. They have insisted that their husbands follow a certain line of activity or enter a certain profession. In such cases, misery abounds. Such women are out of place. They are given over to anxieties and hysterical fears.

The marriage relationship is two sided, and the Word of God is not silent about the obligations of the husband. It does not say as much; it sums it up in a few lines in this chapter. But that by no means implies that the husband's responsibility is not as great.

It is my studied opinion (and I believe that I could prove it statistically if I had kept records over the years) that most marriages fail because the husband refuses to take the place that God intended he should take.

The responsibility for the home, the responsibility for the marriage, and the responsibility for the children, lies in the hands of the man. You have absolutely no right to shove it all off on your wife. You have no right to say to her, "If you were the kind of mother you ought to be, our children would not be in the mess they are in today."

If you think that your wife is not the kind of wife and mother she ought to be, pay attention to the truth of verse 7:

> Likewise, ye husbands, dwell with them according to knowledge, giving honour unto the wife, as unto the weaker vessel, and as being heirs together of the grace of life; that your prayers be not hindered.

The word "knowledge" in the first part of the verse is a translation of the Greek word *gnosis*. This word does not refer simply to knowledge that we may accumulate here and there. Rather, it carries the idea of "experienced knowledge." The construction of the word in the original text suggests "seeking to know." So the message of the verse is: "Dwell with your wife, constantly seeking to know and understand her." Many a man who feels that his wife does not measure up to his expectations would see a tremendous change in her if he himself would make an honest effort to know and to understand her.

One example of how a man can influence the marriage relationship is found in Paul's first letter to the Thessalonians. The significant thing about his advice is that it was written to people who lived in a day much like our own from the standpoint of morals. Marriage vows were not being held as sacred as they should have been. First Thessalonians 4:4 says:

> That every one of you should know how to possess his vessel in sanctification and honour.

An examination of the context in which this verse is found reveals that the word "vessel" refers to the wife. The advice is addressed to the husband. What the Holy Spirit is saying is that as a man seeks to know and to understand his wife, he should pay particular attention to the sexual relationship.

Many of the problems related to broken homes today can be

traced back to the marriage bed. That may not always be the reason given, and it may manifest itself in some other area, but it finds its roots there.

The Word of God makes it very plain that this is the man's responsibility. Men have been known to say: "My problem with my wife is a sexual one. She deceived me before we were married. I thought she was a different kind of person from what she is." The responsibility is still his. God intended that the man be the leader and the teacher, and He intended that you "dwell with your wife according to knowledge"—seeking to know and to understand her.

There are many men today who put much more energy into making their business a success than they do into making their home and marriage a success. There are many men today who spend much time and money acquiring knowledge about various areas of business in which they are interested, who would not walk from one room to another to study the needs of their wives for making their marriage a success. First Peter 3:7 indicates that God expects an entirely different approach. That verse says in part, ". . . giving honour unto the wife as unto the weaker vessel. . . ." The word translated "giving" in that phrase is not the ordinary Greek word for "giving." It is *apomeno,* and it means "to assign a special place." What is the application? It is your responsibility as a husband to dwell with your wife according to knowledge, seeking to know all of her needs and her hopes and her fears, and all the while assigning her a very special place of honor in your life. This is no small task, but this is what God expects the husband to do.

This should serve to illustrate that when God asks a wife to submit herself to her husband, He is definitely not asking her to take an inferior place. He is asking her to take the place that He has ordained for her, and then He goes on to make perfectly clear what that place is. He says it is a place of honor.

In far too many cases the wife loses that place of honor fairly soon after the engagement period ends and the marriage relationship begins. Do you as a husband still open the car door for your wife? Or is it more in keeping with your practice just to pile in and say, "Hurry up. Do you want me to sit here all night?" Do your children hear you when you talk that way? Do you still pull the chair out at the table for your wife as you did when you were engaged? Or do you sit down at the table and yell, "Can't you hurry up? You always bring the biscuits to the table cold."

These may seem to be little things to you, but they serve as a very good index to how much honor your wife receives. Such little details Solomon may have had in mind when he wrote that it is the little foxes that spoil the vines (Song of Sol. 2:15).

There are many illustrations for the word "honor," but it is interesting to notice the ways it is illustrated in the Word of God. In I Peter 1:18-19, there is an illustration that involves a different translation of the word:

> 18 Forasmuch as ye know that ye were not redeemed with corruptible things, as silver and gold, from your vain conversation received by tradition from your fathers;
> 19 But with the precious blood of Christ, as of a lamb without blemish and without spot.

Notice particularly the word "precious" in verse 19. It is a translation of the same Greek word that is translated "honor" in the passage that we have just examined in I Peter 3. How important was the blood of Christ? So important that it was called "precious." God said that this is exactly the way a man ought to feel about his wife. He ought to assign her a place of preciousness, a place of honor.

There is another illustration of this truth in Ephesians 5:25:

> Husbands, love your wives, even as Christ also loved the church, and gave himself for it.

Christ loved the church to the extent that He gave Himself for it. According to this verse, we should love our wives in the same way. As with many of the truths concerning God and His love, our finite minds cannot fully understand this illustration. But in verse 33 of that same chapter there is an illustration that is somewhat easier to comprehend:

> Nevertheless let every one of you in particular so love his wife even as himself; and the wife see that she reverence her husband.

Isn't that a little bit easier to understand? We all love ourselves quite a bit. We pet and pamper and coddle ourselves, and get upset when our wives don't coddle us. This passage of Scripture says that we should love our wives to the same extent as we love ourselves.

There is a further truth taught in I Peter 3:7 related to the husband's responsibility. Not only is he to seek to know and to understand his wife, and not only is he to give her a place of honor and preciousness, but he is also to keep in mind that his relationship to her is to be "as unto the weaker vessel."

A lot of jokes have been built around the statement that the wife is the weaker vessel. Some have referred to it as meaning smaller, or inferior, in size or quality. But the word that is translated "weaker" here is very interesting. It is the Greek word *asthenes,* and it does not refer exclusively to such things as physical or mental condition. It is used more often to express the idea of "delicacy." Actually, this is much more in keeping with the idea that God would have us maintain: "Giving honor unto the wife as unto the more delicate vessel."

Sometimes women are referred to as "high strung." A word that would be much more in keeping with the idea here would be "finely strung." Women have emotional setup that men do not have, and if a man is to dwell with his wife according to knowledge, he must spend time getting to know her delicate emotional setup so that he can indeed assign her a place of honor.

The relationship between the husband and wife is summed up in the phrase "as heirs together of the grace of life." If there is not a togetherness in your spiritual experience, then you will be facing insurmountable problems. Only when there is togetherness in your spiritual experience can you be "heirs together of the grace of life." This may seem far afield from child training. But what could be more basic to child training than the relationship that exists between the child's father and mother?

This passage of Scripture teaches that even if a father and mother pray night and day for their children, they still may not be taking the place that God intended them to take in the home, and their prayers can be and will be hindered in the ways we have discussed. If you pray for your children, yet your children overhear things that lead them to believe that the father does not have the proper respect for the mother, or that the mother does not have the respect she should have for the father, you can pray and pray and pray, and chances are good that you will still have a problem with your children. They sense far more than you think, and they feel far more deeply than you dream possible. They can sense when things are not as they should be between the two of you.

If you want to train your child in the way he should go, remember that you cannot do it without prayer. Also remember that your prayers will be ineffective unless you take the place that God intends for you as husband or wife.

Another requirement for effective praying is that both husband and wife should be Christians. This is why the Bible declares that a person who has put his trust in Christ should not enter into the marriage relationship with one who has not (II Cor. 6:14). It is of the utmost importance—in fact, it is a basic prerequisite for an ideal marriage—that both partners put their trust in the facts that Jesus Christ died for their sins, that He rose from the dead, and that He now lives to intercede with God on their behalf.

7

Disciplining Your Child

The Scriptural basis for our thoughts about child training is found in Proverbs 22:6:

> Train up a child in the way he should go, in keeping with his individual gift or bent, and when he reaches the age of maturity, the time to make his own decisions, he will not depart from the training he has been given.

We have been thinking particularly about the word "train." It is a translation of the Hebrew work *kawnak,* which is translated in a number of different ways in the Scripture. Some of the meanings of this word have already been discussed; others will be discussed later. *Kawnak* is translated as "correction" or "discipline," sometimes used interchangeably, and it is this translation upon which we wish to center our thinking now.

The subject of discipline and correction is discussed in the Bible by the use of three Hebrew words in addition to that of our text. Each of the three words gives a somewhat different meaning to the idea of discipline. They suggest a progression toward maturity in discipline, and we will look at them in that order.

The first two words that are translated "correction"—the word "train" of Proverbs 22:6—are words describing the correction that any parent could make, whether he is saved or unsaved. The type of correction suggested by these two words is the kind that results in obedience, but that is all. It results in compliance with rules, but that is all.

The third word is also translated "correction" in our Bibles, but it is associated with God as well as with man. It speaks of the way God corrects. The secret of discipline and correction is to be able to discipline after the manner in which God disciplines. When we have reached that point in our discipline, then it will be effective.

There are any number of instances in which individuals have held a very stiff rein on their children. Yet as soon as those children had an opportunity, they were disobedient and rebellious and turned away from all their training. Parents who have found themselves in that situation have said, "I do not understand; I held such a stiff rein on them." Others have said, "I do not know what is wrong with my child. I was really strict. Why, I whipped him for disobedience every time he turned around. I do not understand why he has turned against me. I have taught him and I do not know why he has departed from the way." Such problems can be answered by a consideration of what the Scripture says about correction and discipline.

Practically all the passages of Scripture that we will consider are from the Book of Proverbs. This is because the Book of Proverbs was meant not only to help you spiritually, but materially and physically as well.

If we are in good physical health, spiritual victories are more easily won. There is a close connection between the condition of the physical body and the condition of the soul. The Book of Proverbs emphasizes this connection. Spiritual truth is related to physical circumstances. The Book of Proverbs has more to say about child training, about family relationships, and about business success and failure than any other book in the Bible. Therefore, the following verse (Prov. 22:15) is very practical and very material:

> Foolishness is bound in the heart of a child; but the rod of correction shall drive it far from him.

The word "foolishness" is not a word that describes joking or levity. It is a word that describes waywardness. As a matter of fact, it would be closer to the meaning of the verse to say that "waywardness is bound in the heart of a child; but the rod of correction shall drive it far from him." The translators used the word "foolishness" because in the Old Testament a fool is described as a man who does not give God first place in his life.

The word "correction" in this instance is a translation of the Hebrew word *mosayraw,* which describes corporal, or bodily, punishment. The "rod"—the beating, the spanking, the shellacking or however you want to say it—describes the application of the rod. It is a barren word. It does not involve the application of love. It does not involve the use of understanding. It does not involve compassion. It does not involve showing interest. It is an empty, barren word that speaks of securing obedience only by the use of sheer force—securing obedience because you happen to be bigger and older than the child you are punishing. It is obedience demanded by the use of sheer force.

That this word is barren is also indicated by the fact that it is a proper name in Hebrew, as well as an ordinary adjective. It is the name given to a barren place, a wilderness. Much of the correction that many parents administer to their children is as barren as this name implies. There may be love, but the child is not conscious of it. There may be understanding, but the child is not conscious of that understanding. Unfortunately, in too many cases, the love and understanding are absent. The child is corrected only on the basis of "If you do that, I am going to whip you." All he knows is to fear the rod that will be applied if he deviates the slightest degree from what has been laid before him. It is a barren word, and it refers solely to corporal punishment.

It is possible to secure obedience by the use of sheer force, but that kind of correction results in an individual's sitting down on the outside but standing up on the inside. As soon as that individual gets big enough to take the rod out of the hand of the disciplinarian, he will. There are many parents who have to say, "I do not know what to do with my boy; physically, he is too big for me to whip. I cannot whip him, but he needs a whipping." Well, if he needs a whipping by the time he reaches that age, the parents have failed in their training of him. If he needs a whipping by the time he is big enough to take the rod out of their hands, whether they know it or not, they have been *mosayrawing* him—correcting him by sheer force.

Another place where this word is used is Proverbs 15:10:

> Correction is grievous unto him that forsaketh the way: and he that hateth reproof shall die.

The word translated "correction" here is that same word—*mosayraw*. It is significant that the Holy Spirit has been pleased to use it in connection with an individual who has forsaken the way. This is the only kind of correction that people know when they apply the rod and do nothing else. They make no effort to train their child positively. They make no effort to initiate goals and aspirations. All they know is, hold the rod, and when the child forsakes the way, apply the rod. Thus the child lives under a constant threat of corporal punishment.

Perhaps you can begin to see now why an unsaved person could use this type of correction. He does not have to pray when he uses it. All he needs for this type of discipline is a good rod and the strength to use it. He does not have to be concerned about the child's interests. His only thought is, "My child does what I tell him to do or he is in big trouble." That is the kind of correction that is implied by *mosayraw*.

Proverbs 23:13 contains another illustration of the fact that this kind of correction represents only corporal punishment, nothing more:

Withhold not correction from the child: for if thou beatest him with the rod, he shall not die.

And he won't. People who depend solely on the rod rest upon the fact that he won't die.

None of the above should be taken to mean that corporal punishment is wrong. What it does suggest is that corporal punishment can be misused. It will accomplish outward compliance with the rules you have laid down, but it will do so only because you are inflicting physical punishment without understanding, and the child involved will rebel at the first opportunity. One of the big problems that society is facing today is the mistreatment of children. Doctors often treat children for injuries that the parents tell him were suffered when the child fell down the steps or when his playmates walloped him with something. But the doctor knows all the while that this is not the case. He knows it is child abuse.

What is our point? This first word *mosayraw* is the simplest word for correction used in the Bible. It is a kind of correction that is related to physical force, and it will accomplish compliance with the rules, but that is all. At the first opportunity, the recipient of the discipline will rebel.

There is a second word in the Bible that carries the idea of correction. It is the Hebrew word *yawsar*. This word differs from the previous one in that it describes not only blows from a stick but blows from the tongue as well. Sometimes we refer to this as a "tongue-lashing." Anyone who has ever endured a tongue-lashing would agree that, in some instances at least, it would have been more pleasant to endure the blows of a rod. The blows of a rod would have injured the body and eventually the wounds would have healed. But a tongue-lashing injures the spirit, and wounds of the spirit sometimes never heal.

We find another mention of correction in Proverbs 29:17:

> Correct thy son, and he shall give thee rest; yea, he shall give delight unto thy soul.

The word translated "correct" in this verse is *yawsar;* it is not *mosayraw*. It is the word that includes correction with both the rod and the tongue. This is a little better. It is one step higher because, in this instance, the parent is at least taking time to talk to the child. Yet it is still not the best type of correction. It will accomplish some things. In the passages of Scripture to which we have already referred, the rod compels obedience, but that is all. This word does a little bit more: "Correct thy son, and he shall give thee rest." If you yell at him long enough, he will hush; he will quit bothering you. If you get tired of yelling at him, then reach out and belt him. He will get quiet and you will have rest. But the word translated "delight" here is not a word that speaks of happiness. It is a word that describes the idea of not being bothered. It means that you will find a situation where you will not be troubled.

There are any number of parents today who do not emphasize the rod too much, but they are just as cruel with their words as they would be with a stick. In the course of the years I have been in homes where my heart ached when I heard the way parents talked to their children by way of correction. I have watched shadows cross the faces of children when their parents tongue-lashed them in the presence of other people. By this kind of correction, however, the parents accomplish what they set out to do. They have corrected the child and they have peace, and they are able to carry on the conversation that was being interrupted. There is a sort of tranquillity in the home, but there is no tranquillity in the heart of the child. All that this kind of correction accomplishes is the obedience that is demanded, but without any understanding.

This is a little better than the first word, but it still is not the best. An unsaved person could use this method to correct his children. He would accomplish outward compliance.

Now that we have dealt with these two words, let us look at the third word that is translated "correction." The third word is the Hebrew word *yaw-kahh*. This is the word that the Holy Spirit uses when He describes the manner in which God corrects His children. But it is not related exclusively to God; it is used also in connection with parents. If we can learn to correct our children of the flesh as God corrects His children of the spirit, we will know what real correction means.

Have you noticed how many times reference is made in these verses to the fact that the responsibility for discipline lies in the hands of the father? It is the responsibility of the father to be the disciplinarian in the family. What about the mother? She will have practically no disciplining to do if the father has occupied the place that he ought to have. It is the mother's place to nurture, to sustain, and to strengthen. It is the father's place to discipline. However, partnership in discipline cannot be ruled out, because if you should take a concordance and notice the word "parents" as it occurs in the Scripture in connection with discipline, you would find that it is in the plural. So it is a cooperative action. But the place of the father should be emphasized, because all too often the responsibility of discipline is left only in the hands of the mother.

Too often the father says, "I bring in the money, I make the living, and when I come home at night I am tired. I cannot listen to all that talk about the trouble you had with the kids all day long. If you can't control them, it's just too bad; there is nothing I can do about it." If you as a father have that attitude, you are shirking your responsibility.

Do you remember the story of Zipporah, the wife of Moses (Exod. 4)? Just as Moses and his wife were ready to return to Egypt with their children for the purpose of delivering the children of Israel out of the land of Egypt, there was an interruption of the journey. Moses almost died. He would have if his wife Zipporah had not taken their eldest son and circumcised him right then.

Zipporah said to Moses, "You have been a bloody husband to me." What she meant was, "You made me do what you should have done." According to the agreement that God had with Moses, his children were to be circumcised, and he had neglected his duty. If you read the context carefully, you will find that God was going to kill him for his disobedience. But his wife, the mother of his children, took the responsibility that he should have taken, and his life was spared. There are times when a father falls down in his responsibility and the mother has to take over. But it puts a responsibility on her that she has no duty to bear, and God never intended that she should.

Look at these words found in Proverbs 3:

11 My son, despise not the chastening of the Lord; neither be weary of his correction:

12 For whom the Lord loveth he correcteth; even as a father the son in whom he delighteth.

In these two verses there is first a reference to the correction of the child of God by his heavenly Father, and then a reason for the correction. Why does God correct you and me? Because He loves us. He loves us too much to let us be disobedient. God says, "That is how I want you earthly fathers to correct your children. I want you to correct them because you love them. I want you to correct them because your heart is suffused with love for them."

This is the high word, the word that is used of God's discipline. Verse 12 says that correction is given to a son in whom the father delights. The word "delight" in this verse is different from the word "delight" in Proverbs 29:17. Here it is a word that carries a number of ideas. The idea of "admiration" is in this word "delight." You admire your child, his capabilities, his talents, and his abilities. That is why you correct him. You do not want his talents and abilities to go to waste; out of admiration for him, you correct him.

This word "delight" speaks also of satisfaction. Sometimes parents whose children have been reared and now have lives of their own will be heard to say, "You know, my children are such a satisfaction to me." Such parents can rejoice in the successes of their children, whose accomplishments are their parents' accomplishments. That is what is suggested by the word "delight."

The word *yaw-kahh* is used in a number of places in the Word of God, and an examination of some of those verses will help you to understand the attitude of heart that is necessary if you are to discipline your children successfully and train them so that when they are old enough to make their own decisions they will make them along the lines in which they have been trained.

Why do some children, when they are mature enough to make their own decisions, go completely opposite of the way in which they have been trained? At least one reason is that they have been corrected in the wrong fashion. They have been corrected in the manner of the first two words at which we have been looking, and not in the manner of the third.

Job was one of God's children who was corrected. The record of that correction is in the Word of God. This is just another illustration of the marvels of the Word of God, of the inspiration of God's Word, and of how minutely the Holy Spirit has written it. If you want to know how to correct your child, study the Book of Job and see how God corrected Job.

Job's friends, as you know, gave him a lot of advice, good and bad. They did not understand his problem. In chapter 23, Job said:

> 2 Even today is my complaint bitter: my stroke is heavier than my groaning.
> 3 Oh that I knew where I might find him! that I might come even to his seat.
> 4 I would order my cause before him, and fill my mouth with arguments.

The word "arguments" is a translation of our Hebrew word *yaw-kahh,* the word translated "correction" in the previous examples. Now, get the picture. Job was being corrected, and in the midst of it he felt as if he needed to talk to God about it. He said, "If I could, I would fill my mouth with arguments." By that he meant not argumentative discussion, but reasoning and discussion, seeking an understanding.

What can be learned here? When God corrects His children, He permits arguments—reasoning and discussion. When we correct our children, should we not allow time for this same type of reasoning and discussion?

Job continues his thoughts along these lines in verses 5-7:

5 I would know the words which he would answer me, and understand what he would say unto me.

6 Will he plead against me with his great power? No; but he would put strength in me.

7 There the righteous might dispute with him; so should I be delivered for ever from my judge.

Notice the word "dispute" in verse 7. It is the word at which we have been looking, the Hebrew word *yaw-kahh*. What is Job saying? He is saying, "If I could just get an audience with God, I believe I could talk with Him. I believe I could understand what He is trying to tell me." He asks a question, "Will He plead against me with His great power?"—the idea being, since He is God and I am an ordinary mortal, will He just knock me down and say "Be quiet!"? "Oh, no," he says; "no, in such a situation the righteous could reason with Him."

All of this should enforce the idea that if you are going to correct your child, you should correct him with a willingness for discussion about the thing for which you are correcting him. Of course, such discussion is not always necessary. Sometimes you correct your child and the child knows very well why you are correcting him. I am not suggesting that for every time you correct him you have to sit down and go over again the reason why you are correcting him. But you ought to have an open mind and an open heart, and if the child has one sincere question, you ought never to say to him, "You do it because I said so; that is why!" You have no right to say that. If you are going to correct your child as God corrects His children, you must allow time for sincere discussion.

In following this practice, you must remember that children are smart, and sometimes they will ask "Why?" not because they want to know why, but because they just want to postpone doing what you have asked them to do. You have to be wise enough to know when the "Why?" is just a delay tactic and when it is a sincere question that needs an answer. Sometimes when they say "Why?" we have to say to them, "We have been over that already, and you know why." Sometimes we have to say, "I cannot explain to you right now why; you would not understand. Your father knows best."

Sometimes our children have said "Why?" in this way, and we

have said, "All right, sit down and we will tell you why." An example of this is based upon the fact that our children do not go to movies. (If your children do, that is your own business. This is an illustration, not an indictment of movies per se.) Our children do not go. When they were very young and said something about going to a movie, all we needed to say was no, they were not to go to a movie. They did not even ask why. But when they were a bit older, they would ask to go, and we would say, "No, you cannot go to the movies." They would say, "But, Daddy, why?" I could have said, "Because I said so, that's why," but I did not. With each of my children, when he reached the age when he asked the sincere question "Why?" I have sat down with him and said, "This is the reason. You may not be able to appreciate it; you may not be able to understand it; but your daddy has a reason. The reason is that Hollywood as an institution is tearing down everything that your daddy is giving his life to build up. Your daddy teaches from the Word of God that immoral living is wrong, and Hollywood dresses it up and makes it look pretty." I would go on, depending on the age of the child and the need. An important point to remember along this line, incidentally, is that you cannot have a little prepared speech. You have to deal with each question and each child individually. At the conclusion of my reasoning I would say to them, "That is why Daddy cannot let you go to the movies. It would be inconsistent." And that satisfied them. Later they would come along and say, "Daddy, I have some money of my own; I cut the grass, I did some babysitting; I did this or that; I have some money of my own. May I go to the movies with my own money?" I do not bark out and say, "No, you certainly may not!" Rather, I say, "Let's sit down and talk about it." Then I say something like this: "Do you have any idea how much money it takes to buy your clothes and your food and your medicine, and to pay your doctor bills? Do you have any idea?" Readily they say, "A lot, I'm sure." Then I say, "Well, can you pay for those things yourself?" "No, of course not," comes the reply. "Then you really do not have the money to go to the movies. If you were paying for all the things that you need that Daddy has to pay for, you would not have the money to go to the movies. Daddy has already said, remember, that he cannot conscientiously use his money to support an institution that is tearing down everything that he is giving his life to build up.''

The amazing thing is that they accept it. I do not mean to imply that my children would never go to a movie. But they understand why I cannot give them money to go, and they are not bitter about it. And the chances are that when they are on their own, they will choose not to go.

Do you see the point? Whenever you say something to your child by way of correction, you should be willing to talk about it. You should be willing to give a reason. It does not necessarily follow that they will agree with your reason. They may even say, ''Daddy, that doesn't make sense.'' When they say this, and it is a matter of sincere discussion and not a matter of disrespect or rudeness or arguing in an attempt to dissuade you from your purpose—you should take all the time necessary to correct them with understanding. Let them talk about it. Remember, just because you make a statement does not mean that they are going to accept it. If they have reservations, it is far better to let them voice those reservations than for you to be so harsh that they won't tell you what they are thinking.

Another aspect of correction as suggested by this Hebrew word is found in what Job said in chapter 13, verse 15:

> Though he slay me, yet will I trust in him, but I will maintain mine own ways before him.

The word ''maintain'' is a translation of our same Hebrew word *yaw-kahh*. The word ''but'' could be left out of the verse. What Job is saying is, ''No matter what happens to me, I will live consistently before Him.'' Job is talking about consistency. The discipline that will obtain results—the same discipline that God uses with His children—is marked by consistency.

If we as parents fail in one place more often than in another, it is in this matter of consistency. If there is one prayer that my wife and I pray more than any other in regard to our children, it is ''God, help us to be consistent.'' There is nothing any more damaging to children than inconsistency in discipline. It robs them of their confidence in you. They will eventually reach the place where they will not believe what you tell them.

In a public place recently I saw a man with a little child in his arms. The child was probably three years old and was fussing.

They were standing close enough to me that I could not help overhear the whole thing. The child would whine, and the father would say, "I'm going to spank you." The child would say, "No, you are not," and he would whine some more. That went on for ten minutes, and not once did that father spank that child.

He would have been much better off to let the child yell at the top of his lungs than to follow that procedure. I do not know him and I do not know the child, but I can say with certainty that the child is going to be a problem if that practice continues, because he does not believe what his father says.

Perhaps you have had the experience with your own children that when you call them they do not pay any attention. Then you have to raise your voice before they come running. Why do you suppose they do that? It's because you are not consistent. You should not have to raise your voice to a child unless he is so far away that he cannot hear you.

Whether they realize it or not, parents train children in that way. Children are wise. One time when his mother calls him, the child may come. The next time he may say to himself, "Let's see what will happen if I don't answer." If nothing does happen when he doesn't answer the call, he gradually learns that he doesn't need to bother to answer until his mother raises her voice. Inconsistency on the part of parents in maintaining discipline makes liars out of children!

Another illustration of this fact can be taken from my own family. I have never asked my children, "Did you do so-and-so?" They are sons of Adam, and they are sons of Joe Temple. If they think they are going to get into trouble, they could very well be tempted to lie. When we ask, "Did you do it?" they can size up the situation and say to themselves, "Let's see, now, which would be worse: to lie about the situation or to tell the truth and receive some hard punishment?" Sometimes, in such a situation, they might choose to lie. I have always made it a practice to know as many of the facts in the case as I possibly could, and then I would simply say, "Why did you do so-and-so? What is your explanation?"

When my oldest son was a teenager and had just gotten a car, I was pretty sure he had done something he ought not to have done. It was a matter of drag racing and of throwing a few firecrackers on somebody's porch. I heard a rumor that this had happened, so I did a little checking around just to be sure. I did not say a thing to him at that point; he thought everything was just fine and that nobody knew about it. I knew about it for days before I said anything to him about it, because I wanted to be sure. Then, when I felt that I had all the facts straight, I asked him to come into my study, and I said, "I'm sure you have an explanation for everything you do, so I am ready to hear your explanation of why you were drag racing on such and such a street on such and such a night. And I am ready to hear your explanation of why you threw firecrackers on the porch at such and such an address."

By approaching the matter in that way I gave him no opportunity to lie. He knew better than to say, "Dad, I did not do those things." It was obvious that he had been found out. About the drag racing he said, "Dad, I do not have an explanation for it. It is just one of those things. It gets in your blood, and you want to do it, so you do it. I do not have an explanation for it."

I said, "What about the firecrackers?" He said, "Well, there were four other boys in the car, and I was afraid they would call me yellow or a sissy, and all the rest of it. They just talked me into it. That is my explanation for that."

In regard to the drag racing, we had a serious discussion about a lethal weapon in the hands of a young person—or an older person, for that matter—and how easily it can be misused. In regard to his having allowed himself to be talked into doing what he had done, I asked him one question: "Tell me the truth about this. If they had asked you to run down a pedestrian, and had called you a sissy if you refused, would you have run down that pedestrian?" He said, "Of course not!" I said, "Then this reason you have given me is not really a reason, is it?" Sheepishly he replied, "No, Dad, I guess it isn't."

What did we do? Some would say you are not supposed to do anything if the child admits he is wrong. But that is a seriously mistaken idea. Too many people, when they are trying to correct their children, say, "Since he admitted his guilt, I didn't punish him," and the child learns that all he needs to do to escape punishment is to confess (after he has been caught) and act as if he is sorry.

In this instance, we had already set up some rules for the use of the automobile, so I said, "You know what the rules are." He said, "Yes, Dad, I do." I said, "Put the keys on the desk, then." And that was all there was to that particular session.

Consistency. If there is one thing above all other things that I would strive for as a parent, it is consistency.

Another illustration of this same point concerns a mother with whom I counseled who had been very, very strict with her daughter until the girl reached the teenage years. But when that girl reached her teens, the mother completely reversed herself about every rule she had ever made. That girl wound up on the couch of a psychiatrist. Sometime later, the girl told her mother, "When you took off those restrictions, it was just as though you said to me, 'I have been wrong all these years.' At that critical age when I needed guidance and direction, it was as though you admitted that you did not know what it was all about. You changed."

This is the inevitable result of a lack of consistency: It will confuse your child. He may chafe under correction, he may dislike the restriction, but it gives him an anchor to hold to. He can always say, "Mom and Dad are right; I do not like it, but they are right."

Isaiah 1:18 gives us still another translation of the Hebrew word *yaw-kahh:*

> Come now, and let us reason together, saith the Lord: though your sins be as scarlet, they shall be as white as snow; though they be red like crimson, they shall be as wool.

Here *yaw-kahh* is translated "reason," and it suggests a very important element of correction. This is reasoning on the part of the parent. We have been talking about the child's stating his position, and your listening as a parent. But reasoning is two sided; there is reasoning that a parent must do.

This reasoning involves pointing out to the child the error of his way, making clear to him the direction in which he is headed, and being able to prove your point. A word of caution is in order: Do not ever get yourself out on a limb. Be very sure that you can prove that point. Do not ever make a statement to your child that he knows is false and that you deep down inside know is false. Do not ever make a statement to your child that you know very well you cannot prove or explain, because in all probability he, too, knows that you cannot prove it. Your child is practical and he is smart, and it won't be long until he realizes that your discipline is not based on reason, but is based on a few peculiar ideas that you have and that you want to force on him. He will not like that any more than you would like it. He will chafe under it.

Take time to reason with your children. Keep in mind that there is a difference between "talking back" and "reasoning." Never allow your child to talk back, but take advantage of every opportunity to point out to your child the good and the bad of certain things. Give him reasons.

How many Christian mothers have said to their daughters, "Don't you let that boy get you into trouble." It depends entirely upon her associations whether or not that girl has any idea what her mother is talking about, because if her mother has not reasoned with her, it is very possible that all she knows about sex she has learned in the wrong fashion, and her ideas may be confused and distorted.

How much better it would be for that mother to reason with her daughter, and to show her that the body is the temple of the Holy Spirit; that it is not a matter of getting into trouble (although that is involved if the girl is too familiar with a boy) but rather a matter of desecrating the body in which the Holy Spirit has delighted to dwell.

Sometimes when we reason with our children in this way, we wonder whether or not we are getting across. But here is an illustration of how well it works: One year during Easter vacation, one of our daughters went to visit her brother and sister who were attending a Christian university. It was the first time she had traveled alone. She was a little panicky, and her mother and I were more so. Because she is a very attractive girl, I was not at all surprised when she came home and told us that on the plane a sailor came and sat down beside her almost immediately. I said, "Tell me about it." She said, "He sat down, and in a few minutes the hostess came by and asked if we wanted something to drink." She told the hostess she did not want anything, but the sailor said, "Yes, I will have a cocktail." Then he said to my daughter, "Are you sure you don't want a cocktail?" She said, "No, I don't believe I do." When he had his drink in hand, he turned to her again and said, "Do you think I ought not to drink this?" She replied, "Well, it's your life." A little bit later, as the conversation progressed, he said, "Give me a good reason why I shouldn't drink this." She said, "You answer a few questions for me first. Are you a Christian?" He said, "Yes, I am a Christian; sure I am a Christian." She said, "If you are a Christian, you have the answer. Your body is the temple of the Holy Spirit, and you have no right to defile it by drinking or in any other way." His reply was, "Good gosh, where did you hear something like that?" Then to me she said, "I remember hearing you say that just two or three weeks ago, Daddy, and I told him that."

Incidentally, when they were ready to get off the plane he said, "I guess if I had not had that cocktail, I could have a date with you tonight, couldn't I?" You see, we do not need to be afraid that when our children use the reasoning they have been taught by adults, they will be rejected by their peers.

My daughter got the point of my reasoning. It was not a matter of whether you drink or don't drink. It is a question of your body's being occupied by the Holy Spirit.

I could have told my daughter simply not to drink because she might become an alcoholic, and she might have told me that she would take that chance. But if you can get your child to realize that his body is the temple of the Holy Spirit, there will be many things that you won't have to worry about.

Of all the verses that describe this type of correction, Job 9:33 is by far the most important. If you implement these other suggestions and yet fall down here, you will fail:

> Neither is there any daysman betwixt us, that might lay his hand upon us both.

These words were spoken when Job felt as if he were utterly alone. He said, "If there were just somebody to intercede, if there were a daysman, if there were a go-between, if there were a mediator, if there were just somebody to intercede between me and God, everything would be all right."

Look at the word "daysman." It is a translation of the word *yah-kahh,* and it suggests a final aspect of discipline. Your correction, if it is to accomplish the purpose that it should accomplish, must be infused with the ministry of intercession. By means of prayer you should be a "daysman." You should stand between your child and God, not in the sense that your child does not need to be born again—he certainly does—but in the sense that you can intercede in his behalf.

The first chapter of the Book of Job tells us that, according to custom, Job offered an animal sacrifice yearly for all his children. He said, "I do not know. Maybe they have done something to displease God. I hope they haven't, but maybe they have. To be sure, I am going to offer this sacrifice."

I spend a great deal of time in prayer for my own children. But I do not let praying take care of it all. This is not to suggest that you should spend all of your time in prayer and not give your children any training. Even while I am making every effort to train them along the lines we have discussed, I spend a great deal of time interceding for them. It is amazing what that can do!

8

Restricting Your Child

Thus far our basic study has centered around the first word of Proverbs 22:6. The word is "train," and it is a translation of the Hebrew word *kawnak,* the basic meaning of which is "discipline" or "correction."

To determine the exact meaning of the statement about child training in Proverbs 22:6, we have noticed that there are three other words in the Hebrew language that are translated "correction" in the Bible, and we have examined each of them. One of them is correction related solely to corporal punishment; another is related to the spoken word along with corporal punishment. The third word, which bespeaks the highest type of correction, is related to a spoken word along with corporal punishment, but it includes more than those two factors. It is a correction that deals with the whole personality. It does not enforce obedience simply by physical coercion.

Now let us continue to examine this word "train" because it has some other meanings, and we will not be able to understand fully what it means to train a child on the basis of this verse unless we understand the other basic meanings of the word *kawnak.* Another meaning of the word is "narrow."

That is a word that could speak volumes to us from a number of different standpoints. Basically, the first word that comes to our minds when we think of the word "narrow" is "restriction." If your children are at an age when they can discuss things with you, and if you have placed any restrictions on them at all, probably you have heard them say to you, "You are too narrow." They do not want to be restricted. The successful method of training a child so that he won't say this of you is to have good reasons for your restrictions, and to let him know those reasons.

You recall that we said we should train the child according to his individual bent. We suggested that the personality or nature of the child is shaped by three things. It is shaped in a general way toward evil because of what we referred to as "Adam's sin." It is shaped in a specific way toward evil because of what we referred to as "great-great-grandfather's sin" or "grandfather's sin." Then it is shaped in a specific way toward good because of the intricate work that God performs in the human embryo before it is ever brought to birth.

It is important to know and understand your child on the basis of these things. Because the personality of your child is bent according to Adam's nature and according to a particular weakness toward evil that he has inherited from his own family, it is necessary to place restrictions on him if he is to be trained properly.

There are several illustrations of this in the Word of God. For example, in I Peter 2:11 we read:

> Dearly beloved, I beseech you as strangers and pilgrims, abstain from fleshly lusts, which war against the soul.

The phrase in which we are interested is "abstain from fleshly lusts, which war against the soul." You might be inclined to say, "What does that have to do with child training?"

The word translated "abstain" here means literally "to hold off from." The lusts of the flesh, like an encamped army, are making war against the soul. If that is an address to Christian people, think how much easier it will be for your child, when he becomes a Christian, if you have so trained him in regard to these fleshly lusts that he already knows, in some measure, how to cope with them.

We are not ruling out the power of the Holy Spirit. The Holy Spirit indwells our bodies, but the war that He makes against sin is made through human instrumentality. If we present to the Holy Spirit at the time of a child's regeneration a body that is well trained, the battle will not be nearly so great.

Some restrictions have to be placed around your child in view of the fact that he has Adam's nature. He will "do what comes naturally" unless there are definite restrictions made.

I remember spending nearly a whole day dealing with a mother and father who had a serious problem with one of their children. Their oldest daughter was in her last year of high school. She married a boy secretly at the beginning of the semester, and when her parents learned of it they did the only thing they could do as parents; they tried to make the best of the situation. The young couple, however, after living together just a few weeks, decided to break up their marriage. The boy joined the army, and the girl went back home. When they came to me, these parents were broken-hearted because their daughter was pregnant by another boy and still had three weeks left in high school. She is a Christian girl, and she was reared in a Christian home. She was not from "the wrong side of the tracks." She and her family were considered the highest type of people morally. The questions bothering these parents were: "Where did we fail?" "Where did we go wrong?" "We trusted her." "We did not dream she would ever do a thing like this."

They had another girl a few years younger, and an additional reason why they were so concerned, aside from the fact that they needed advice about the expected baby, was that they did not want to repeat the same tragic mistake. So they asked, "Where did we fail?"

I told them, "I do not know all the details, of course, but you have made one statement in the course of this conversation that gives me a clue as to where you have made at least one mistake. That statement is 'We trusted her. We did not think she would ever do anything like this.' "

Quickly these folks said, "Don't you trust your daughters?" I said, "Yes, very much. But I do not trust the nature with which they were born. You have made a very grave mistake in thinking that your daughter can spend her time parked in an automobile on a country road hour after hour, night after night, and escape this thing that has happened."

Do you see the point I am making? That is the only reason I have brought up this sad illustration. The Bible says, "Abstain from fleshly lusts, which war against the soul." You and I as parents must place around our children certain restrictions that will enable them to fight the battle against lusts, which are like a mighty army encamped around the soul, waiting to destroy it, to bring about its downfall.

In I Thessalonians 5:22 is another suggestion that emphasizes what we are discussing and adds a little additional light. This verse makes an even more definite suggestion to us as parents:

Abstain from all appearance of evil.

The word translated "abstain" here is exactly the same as the one used in I Peter; it means "to hold off." But the word "appearance" is a translation of the Greek word *eidos,* which suggests the idea of form, of fashion, or of shape. This passage of Scripture says, then, "Abstain from every form, every fashion, every shape, of evil."

If we think about this from a parental standpoint, it suggests that we should so restrict our children that they will not be coming in constant contact with the shapes, forms, and fashions of evil.

Do not jump to conclusions and say, "That is an utter impossibility. You can overprotect your child." But we will answer that before we are through with this discussion.

What we are thinking about now is the meaning of the word "train." It means "narrow," and restrictions are suggested by that word. As parents, we should place restrictions upon our children in regard to habits, as is suggested in I Peter 2:11. Instead of asking the Lord to deliver the child from some habit after it has already been established, we should see to it that bad habits are not formed in the first place.

I personally do not believe, for example, that smoking is a good habit. I do not preach against it; I preach the Word of God. I do not fuss at anybody who does smoke. That is one's own personal responsibility. If somebody says, "Excuse me, I want to smoke," I usually say, "You do not need to excuse yourself; just help yourself." I believe that is a personal liberty that belongs to everybody; but I still do not feel that it is a good habit. I think that anyone would agree with me that it certainly is not a good habit for children and youth. I have never seen the point in letting children develop some bad habit and then being exceedingly burdened about it after they have acquired it.

Smoking is one habit that seems particularly attractive to young people. My father lived with us for ten years before his death, and he smoked all the time. Again, that was his business. But he used to say to my oldest son, "Why don't you smoke with me?" The boy would say, "No, I don't think I should." My father would say, "Go ahead. I won't tell your dad about it." So in this instance the pressure to smoke was brought right in our home. You are aware from your own experience how it is brought in from the outside. Then, too, there is always the matter of young people trying their wings to show how "mature" they are.

One evening when my son was washing his hands at the lavatory, I stepped into the bathroom since the door was open. The lavatory was rather high, and at that time he was rather short. He had to stretch up to reach the lavatory, and when he did the sport shirt that was over his breeches rose, and a package of cigarettes in his back pocket came into view.

I am not going to say that I just "happened in" about that time. I have asked the Lord to keep me in touch with my children, and I try to keep in touch with them. I believe that if you pray that way, the Lord will let you know things you ought to know. He will arrange your schedule so that you just "happen in" at the right time, if you depend on Him to do it.

So when my son was washing his hands, and the cigarettes were in evidence, I said, "I suppose we have something to talk about, don't we?" He looked at me for just a moment, and then the light of comprehension spread across his face. "Well, Dad," he said, "I guess we do." So we went into my study, and I said, "Would you like to tell me about what is in your back pocket?" He knew that there was no point in arguing, so he laid the cigarettes on the desk. I said, "How did you get them?" "I lied," he said. "I went down to the grocery store on the corner, and I told the man they were for Granddad, and he sold them to me."

"We have talked about this before, have we not?" I said. "Yes," came the reply, "we have." So I said, "We are not going to break a habit after it gets started. We are going to stop it before it starts."

I may have sounded earlier in this discussion as if I do not believe in corporal punishment, because I was emphasizing that there is something more to punishment than the physical aspect.

But I do believe in it. I have not had to administer it very often, but when I have to administer it, I do.

I do not have a verse of Scripture for what I am saying now; it is the way the Lord has led me, and I offer it here for whatever it may be worth. Whenever I have had to administer any corporal punishment to my children, I have endeavored to do more than just irritate them. I have been in homes where, in administering punishment, the parents did nothing more than irritate the children; that is all. It is just a slap on the wrist; that is all. That is wasted time and effort.

We have always had this arrangemnt: Our children will go into their individual rooms, and I will come in later at a stated time. I do not mean that I stay away deliberately to make them suffer and wonder what is going to happen. They know what is going to happen. I stay away long enough that they will know, and I will know, that the punishment is not being administered just because I am angry. At that particular time I used the rod (Prov. 13:24) in the manner in which I felt the disobedience required.

Then I said this to my son, because, remember, he was quite young at this time—I have said this to all my children, incidentally—"Now you can cry if you want to because it is not pleasant to be punished. But we are not having any sulkiness and we are not having any screaming and we are not having any tantrums." Then I left the room. At the time of this writing, my son is thirty years of age, and by his own declaration he has never smoked another cigarette.

Once I overheard him talking to some boys about how he broke the habit of smoking. He did not know that I was overhearing, but he said, "I'll tell you, fellows, I did not have to break the habit. My Dad broke it for me after the first cigarette. I never see a cigarette in anybody's mouth that I don't think about that experience."

That is just an illustration. The same procedure may not work at all in your case, but the point I am making concerns the word "train," it concerns the word "narrow," and it concerns the habits and lusts that war against the soul. You and I as parents have a responsibility to make a narrow path for our children by the use of restrictions that relate to abstaining from the very appearance of evil, as we read in I Thessalonians 5:22. As parents we have a responsibility to restrict our children so that they will have some help in this battle against the flesh.

For that reason I restrict the kinds of programs my children watch on television. If they went to movies, I would certainly restrict the kinds of movies they would see; there is ample room for restriction there. I even restrict the kinds of magazines they read. For example, when my children were smaller, they all liked comic books. We tried to be very careful about the types of comic books they bought. There are a lot of things being published misleadingly as comic books and which create a problem that we may not recognize at first. They understood that they were not to buy anything but a certain type of comic book that would pass the rule we had set down.

We even restrict the kind of music they play on the stereo. I see no point in asking God to make your children spiritual and yet giving them money to buy music that appeals to nothing above the belt and to everything below it. It is utter foolishness to say, "God, help my child to be spiritual," and then put him in an atmosphere where it will be a superhuman task for him to be spiritual.

Notice the words of I Corinthians 15:33:

> Be not deceived: evil communications corrupt good manners.

This is a very important verse in relation to the boundaries of restriction in another area of our children's lives. The word "communications" is a translation of the Greek word *homilia,* and a better translation might be "associations." Do not let yourself be deceived; evil associations corrupt good manners. The phrase "good manners" is a translation of the Greek word *ethos,* which would be better translated "good moral habits." There you have the meaning of the verse: "Be not deceived: evil associations corrupt good moral habits."

This verse, therefore, suggests that we have a responsibility to restrict the associations that our children have. Your child may already say you are narrow. If you follow through with this, there may even be some adults who will say that you are narrow, and who may be offended at you. But I believe that as parents interested in the training of our children, we should know with whom they associate. If there is a need for restriction, we should not hesitate to order the restriction regardless of whom it may hurt or whom it may offend.

In our day there is perhaps more need for this than ever before. You probably have had experience with "slumber parties," for example. There are a lot of problems that arise at slumber parties. If you could overhear some of the conferences I have had with mothers about their daughters who have attended slumber parties, you would never let your child attend one without knowing something about the associations there.

Will you notice what I said? I did not say that you should never let them attend. I said you should never let them attend without knowing something about the associations.

When our children attend slumber parties, if my wife has not met the mother in the home where the party is to be, she either goes to meet her or calls her on the phone and talks with her. Of course she does not make herself offensive by saying, "Now look; my daughter was invited to a slumber party at your house, and I want to know if it is a fit place for her to come." But she does find out who will be at the slumber party and how the party will be chaperoned, and her decision on whether or not the girls are to be allowed to attend is based on those things.

It is rather foolish to get all upset when your children acquire some bad habits after you have not taken the time to consider with whom they are associating or to be concerned about the habits they would acquire if they associated with certain people.

I had a conference recently with some parents who were among the sponsors of a band trip from one of our local high schools. These parents were very concerned since some of the students had to be sent home because they had liquor with them on the bus. They were also distressed because in the hotel the boys and girls went to each others' rooms dressed in their night clothes. They were also very much concerned because some of the girls disrobed on the bus in the process of changing clothes. Some of the other sponsors, when an investigation was made, said that the students had acted like perfect ladies and gentlemen. These parents said to me, "The thing that really concerns us is, what can we do about it? It seems that there is nothing we can do."

I said, "I do not think that there is anything you can do about it.

This probably is not the first time it has happened. It is just the first time you have heard about it. As long as there are parents who think that such actions are the actions of ladies and gentlemen, you will not be able to do anything about it."

Then the mother said, "What shall I do about sending my son on the next band trip?" To see what these parents, husband and wife, would say, I said, "You mean to tell me that you do not trust him?" This mother and father were among the few parents with whom I have talked who have given an intelligent answer to such a question. They said, "We trust him, but we do not know how strong he is. We do not know, if he goes on a trip where that sort of thing occurs, whether he could withstand it. He may take his first drink on that trip. What are we to do?"

They made the suggestion that perhaps they could force the school to stop sponsoring band trips altogether, which of course was naive. I said in response to that, "You cannot be responsible for everybody else's children. You can be responsible only for your own. If I were you, I would volunteer to be sponsor for the next band trip, for the sake of my own children." They said, "They won't have us again; they have already told us that." "Then I would find out who the sponsors are to be," I said, "and I would find out what their moral standards are. If they are sponsors who think it is ladylike and gentlemanly to drink and to be in improper attire before the opposite sex, I would say to my son, 'You are not going on that band trip.' "

Immediately these parents said, "If we did that, he would fail his band course." "That remains to be seen," I said; "but if he does fail his band course, that is just one of the prices that Christian parents sometimes have to pay if they want to train their children properly."

I want to emphasize that, because if you are not willing to pay the price to train your child in line with what you believe the Word of God teaches, you had better not start out this way in the first place. You may well be asked to pay a price sometime before it is all over.

We have already said that this matter of restriction is related to the way in which your individual child is bent, and we have been looking at it from the standpoint of what we have referred to as the

"Adamic nature." But we also said that your child is bent toward that which is good. God has a plan and purpose for him. The question is often asked, "How do we know that plan? How do we know that purpose?" The answer generally given is that all we can do is pray about it and to seek the mind of the Lord, to ask God to make us alert to the tendencies toward good and the tendencies for talent that we may see in our child. This we know—that the goal for every child is a personal relationship with Jesus Christ.

You cannot make that decision for your child; you cannot force him into the decision. But it is senseless to think of rearing children just hoping that they will come to a saving knowledge of Jesus Christ. It should not even be considered.

The Bible very plainly says that it is not God's will that any should perish, but that all should come to repentance (II Peter 3:9). I know that when I pray according to the will of God, He is going to answer my prayers. I have prayed for all of my children that they will come to a saving knowledge of the Lord Jesus Christ. Thank God, by His grace they have. That is the ultimate goal.

If I know that they are going to be Christians, and if I know, for example, that God may have some special purpose for them in life, I should train them with that purpose in mind, and I should control their associations with that purpose in mind. This does not mean that I think that all my children ought to preach or go into the mission field. I do not believe that there are compartments of Christian service. An individual who is born again belongs to God, and whatever demand God makes on him is the demand that he should fulfill. But if the ultimate goal in the training of your child is that he come to a saving knowledge of Jesus Christ, then you should train him with a view to the Christian experience he is going to have by and by.

Perhaps a word of caution is in order. A number of times I have talked with young people who have been reared in Christian homes and whose parents have been faithful about their training, so that when they came to a saving knowledge of Christ there was not a great, dramatic, climactic change in their lives. They would begin to wonder whether they had been born again. They would sometimes wonder whether they had really had an experience of grace in their hearts.

This is one reason why I personally am opposed to any visiting evangelist giving his life story. I have never been interested, in any place I have pastored, in hearing a long, drawn-out story about how someone lived so many years as a drunkard and so many more years as a gambler and so many more years as a member of Al Capone's gang and all the rest of it, and then having a flock of young people come up afterward and say, "I do not know whether I am saved or not. Brother So-and-So said he had a great change in his life, but there has been no great change in my life." We have to explain, "Of course there was not. You were not doing the things he did, thank God. There did not need to be as great a change in your life."

If we train our children with the goal of their ultimately accepting Christ as their personal Savior, then we will want to restrict them in accordance with that goal.

Second Corinthians 6:14-18 emphasizes another aspect of this truth:

> 14 Be ye not unequally yoked together with unbelievers: for what fellowship hath righteousness and unrighteousness? and what communion hath light with darkness?
> 15 And what concord hath Christ with Belial? or what part hath he that believeth with an infidel?
> 16 And what agreement hath the temple of God with idols? for ye are the temple of the living God; as God hath said, I will dwell in them, and walk in them; and I will be their God, and they shall be my people.
> 17 Wherefore come out from among them, and be ye separate, saith the Lord, and touch not the unclean thing; and I will receive you,
> 18 And will be a Father unto you, and ye shall be my sons and daughters, saith the Lord Almighty.

Verses 15 through 18 are a commentary on verse 14, the statement in which we are interested:

> Be ye not unequally yoked together with unbelievers. . . .

God means what He says. It does not mean that a Baptist ought not to marry a Methodist. It does not mean that a Methodist ought not to marry a Roman Catholic, if the Catholic is a believer in Christ. But it does mean that a believing child of God, a born-again believer, ought not to marry an unbeliever. It means that a believer ought not to be linked with an unbeliever in any type of permanent association.

If you know that your child ultimately will be a child of God —and I reemphasize that I would consider nothing else—I would not wonder whether or not my child was going to be saved; I would know he was going to be saved, and I would not let God alone until he was. If you know that your child is going to be a born-again believer, would it not be wise to restrict his associations in these early years, so that he will not be exposed to the danger of sin after he becomes a believer?

I mentioned that our children have all received the Lord as their personal Savior. We have daughters of dating age. Our daughters know that they may not date an unbeliever for any length of time. This does not mean that every time someone asks them for a date they say, "Now sit down, because I have a few questions I want to ask you. First of all, are you a Christian?" I do not mean that. There are any number of reasons why they might have a date for only one particular event. But our daughters know that there is no point in their accepting dates with an unbeliever on an extended basis.

Our daughters have not had dates repeatedly with boys without our having a discussion with them as to whether or not the boys are born-again believers. I have had so many people come to me and say, "Will you pray about my daughter, will you pray about my son? He [or she as the case may be] is going to marry somebody who is not a Christian." Sometimes, if I know the people well enough and because I want to make a point, I say to them, "Oh, when did they start going together? Last night?" Usually the reply is something like this: "Of course not! They have been going together for two years." Then I say, "Why are you just now getting so concerned about it?" You see, it is too late after the wedding date has been set to begin to ask God to keep your girl or your boy from marrying an unbeliever. You ought to stop it before it ever gets started. If it is not pleasing to God for believers to marry unbelievers, and if your child is going to be a believer, why should you do anything to encourage something displeasing to Him?

I personally will not knowingly perform a marriage ceremony for a believer and unbeliever. I say "knowingly" because there have been a few times when I have been fooled, if I can judge by later results. The reason I won't do it is that God's Word says that a believer and an unbeliever should not be yoked together, and I will not knowingly be a party to violating God's Word. On the same principle, you should guard the associations of your children so that they will not be in constant company with unbelievers.

I hope that you will never fall for one of the slickest lies the devil has ever told. It is that your girl or your boy who associates with an unbeliever can bring that unbeliever to a saving knowledge of Christ. That is a lie of the devil! I am not referring to giving a witness to someone. I am not speaking of a Christian child or teenager going to great lengths to expose one of his friends to the gospel. I am speaking of keeping constant, extended company with an unbeliever. Generally speaking, it just does not work. In those rare cases where it has worked, it has been by the grace of God and nothing more.

A young lady once told me, "I have prayed about this, and God has told me to let my boy friend give me an engagement ring, because God wants me to win him to the Lord." I said, "No, God did not tell you that." "Well, I prayed about it," she said. I said, "Then you heard someone besides the Lord, because God does not contradict Himself. If God tells you not to be yoked with an unbeliever, He is not going to tell you to be engaged to that boy so that you can lead him to Christ." That has led as many people astray as any other one lie that I know anything about.

Look at the words of I Corinthians 6:19-20:

> 19 What? know ye not that your body is the temple of the Holy Ghost which is in you, which ye have of God, and ye are not your own?
> 20 For ye are bought with a price: therefore glorify God in your body. . . .

The verse should stop there. The last part of that verse, "and in your spirit," is not in the original text. It is unfortunate that it is in the translation because it waters down the whole meaning of the verse.

These verses do not speak of glorifying God in your spirit; they speak of glorifying God in your body. When the word "spirit" is added, it sidetracks our attention from the main subject.

Here is a definite statement that you and I as believers are to glorify God in our body because our physical body is the temple of the Holy Spirit. I hope you are thinking with me. Ultimately, your child, though he may be a babe in arms at the moment, is going to be a Christian. There is no excuse for his not being one. And it will be his responsibility to glorify God in his body, because the Holy Spirit is going to take up residence there. There are a lot of Christians who have been believers for years who do not know this truth. They do not know that they have a responsibility to glorify God in their bodies.

How wonderful it would be if we could train our children in such a fashion, even before they become Christians, that the moment they are born again they would realize that their bodies are the temple of the Holy Spirit and that they should glorify God in their bodies.

If you are to train your child in that way, you must train him in some very practical things that may bring you in for real criticism and may give him a difficult time. It would be impossible to apply this to all the details that may present themselves, but there are two illustrations that emphasize the principle. Then you can make the application to any number of other things. First, notice the apostle Paul's instructions in I Timothy 2:9-10:

> 9 In like manner also, that women adorn themselves in modest apparel, with shamefacedness and sobriety; not with braided hair, or gold, or pearls, or costly array;
> 10 But (which becometh women professing godliness) with good works.

Some of the statements in these verses are relative. The relative statements involve the time in which Paul lived; the original statement involves principle. The principle is that women should adorn themselves in modest apparel. The little girls of today will be the women of tomorrow. God says that He expects Christian women to adorn themselves in modest apparel. Let us think about the word "modest" for a moment. I hope you won't accept the common, ordinary meaning of the word "modest." If you do, then you will date yourself to a particular era, and instead of presenting a modest testimony you will present a peculiar figure.

The word "modest" is a translation of the Greek word *kosmos,* and what it literally means is "an orderly arrangement." The principle stated here is: "Let women adorn themselves in a manner that is orderly." There are, for example, some Christian parents who do not feel that their daughters should wear shorts and slacks. They rule them out completely. This is not to be critical of those parents; it is merely an illustration. Such parents feel that anybody who dresses in that fashion is dressing immodestly. That is because they are looking at the word "modest" according to the era and not according to the principle.

An attitude more in keeping with what the Scripture says is that there is an orderly arrangement that should be followed in one's clothing. There is a place for girls to wear pants. In fact, if you are going to hew to the line about modesty, pants or jeans are much more modest in some sports events than are skirts and dresses. But Main Street is no place for pants. Church is no place for pants. Pajamas are perfectly all right in the bedroom, but you are not to have them on at a party. There is an orderly arrangement involved regarding clothes.

Shorts are appropriate in some places. They are entirely inappropriate if it is a matter of displaying physical attractiveness before men whose eyes are already filled with lust.

So when we think about modest apparel, let us think of it as orderly arrangement. If you have daughters in your home, teach them from the very beginning that certain clothes are proper in certain places for certain purposes. Then when they become teenagers, you will not have as much of a problem about their being improperly dressed. You won't be stopping something after it has started. You will have stopped it before it ever got started.

My wife and I have prayerfully made decisions about what we think is an orderly arrangement of clothing for our daughters. We have been criticized in some instances for what they have worn. I remember an incident, for example, when I was having a conference with a woman in my study in my home, and one of my daughters breezed by the room wearing shorts. The conference was brought to a sudden conclusion. I was given a very sound lecture about how my testimony was hurt and my influence curtailed because my daughter wore shorts.

What this dear lady did not take the trouble to understand was that my daughter was in her own home. She did not take the time to understand that we have specific rules and regulations about clothing that we believe are in line with the Scripture. But her reaction did not bother me in the least. If I know that I am doing what I should be doing, according to God's direction and according to His words, then—I hope you don't misunderstand this—frankly, I could not care less what people think. You cannot regulate your activities by the inclinations of individuals. If you do, you will be changing your standards every time somebody turns around.

The word *kosmos* that we are thinking about applies to boys as well as to girls, but not so much from the standpoint of "orderly arrangement." You cannot expect orderly arrangement from most boys! Until they reach a certain age, their clothes probably will be disarrayed and will not match. But this word involves the idea of tidiness, and it involves the idea of taking care of one's person.

It is a very grave mistake to fail to teach your son (this would apply in many instances to a daughter as well) habits of personal hygiene. You will have a real problem on your hands when he gets old enough to embarrass you by the way he looks. If you start out early in life, however, he will have developed habits that will already be in force, and you won't be like the television commercial you see in which the mother, frustrated, says, "He did not brush his teeth again!"

In the early days it may be a real problem; you may almost despair about tooth brushing and the rest of it, but the time will come when the habit will be acquired. You say, "What does all this have to do with training our child for the Lord, and according to his individual bent?" It has this to do with it: Christian testimony falls down in the matter of good grooming as often as in any other area. If we have a glowing Christian testimony it can be made more so if we are tidy about our persons, and if our appearance is everything that it ought to be.

The word *kosmos* also means "to take care of." We should instruct our sons to take care of their bodies, not only by physical exercise but in all the problems that young men face in the process of growing up. If we teach them the meanings of this word to begin with, we won't have to deal with a lot of problems later on. Some of the problems that psychiatrists are having to deal with today in young men could have been avoided. Notice that I said *some* could have been avoided, if parents had been faithful in their training in these areas.

There is another verse that gives us an illustration in addition to I Timothy 2:9, 10. You will find it in Deuteronomy 22:5. (You may be inclined to think that we are straining a point in emphasizing this verse, but remember, we are not trying to deal with all the problems; we are simply giving some illustrations.)

> The woman shall not wear that which pertaineth unto a man, neither shall a man put on a woman's garment: for all that do so are an abomination unto the Lord thy God.

That means exactly what it says. On one occasion when I was dealing with this verse, someone, supposedly with a great degree of intelligence, said to me, "That verse does not have any application now, because when that verse was written, the men wore skirts and the women wore pants. It has no application at all." But this is a principle; it is not a verse related to any particular era. It might just as well say, "In whatever era you live, a woman shall not wear that which pertaineth to a man, neither shall a man put on a woman's garment. . . ." It is my opinion that we should take this verse of Scripture literally.

I say this in all seriousness. I think it is a very grave mistake for parents to let little boys dress like girls and play with dolls beyond a certain age. You could well be allowing a tendency with which a psychiatrist will have to deal in later years. On the other hand, girls ought not to be permitted to wear men's clothing, not so much because a psychiatric problem will result, but because God's Word says they should not. Somebody says, "That is exactly why I do not let my girls wear slacks." Now wait just a moment. The verse says that no woman should wear anything that pertaineth to a man. I do not believe that there is any normal man who would be caught dead in a pair of women's slacks. By the farthest stretch of your imagination you could not call them men's clothing. They belong to women; they are designed and made for women. So to say that this applies to slacks does not necessarily follow.

You say, "Then there is no problem." Yes, there is, because we are living in a world that is dedicated to fashion. If you have not already experienced a problem with your daughters along this line, you will. They want what they want for no other reason than that fashion demands it. This verse is an illustration in point.

Some time ago in the high school that my daughter attended there was a custom that all the girls should come to school in jeans on a certain day. That in itself would not have been so terrible. But these had to be boys' jeans. One of my daughters came home and said, "Daddy, I need some new jeans." I said, "What happened to the ones you had?" She said, "Oh, they are just fine, but I need some new ones." "Why do you need new ones?" I asked. This was her reply: "We are all going to wear boys' jeans to school." So we sat down and discussed the situation. Of course she brought out the arguments that are always presented; there is no use to repeat them in detail: Everybody's doing it, and if I don't do it I will be thought peculiar, etc., etc., etc.

I opened the Word of God to this verse, and I said, "Every decision that we have made, we have tried to make on the authority of the Word of God. Sometimes we have been wrong in the decisions we have made because we have not had all the information. When we have been wrong in a decision, we did not hesitate to back down. But when we make a decision that is based on the Word of God, and we know that we are correct about it, that decision is going to stand even if you are the only one in the whole school who does not have on boys' jeans." And the matter was settled.

Now do not misunderstand. I said the matter was settled; I do not mean that everybody was happy. But we were not trying to make everybody happy; we were trying to settle the matter. But this is what I am stressing: If we train our children according to the Word of God, it will sometimes be necessary to put restrictions on them in the light of God's Word. You may have to take a stand and be considered narrow by your children, by their associates, and even by the parents of other children. But if you are to train your child according to God's intended plan for him, restriction at times will be an absolute necessity.

9

Initiating Your Child

The subject of placing restrictions on children is not popular. It is contrary to much of what psychologists tell us today about child training. Many parents are reluctant to place restrictions on their children because, it is said, that is a negative approach.

A negative approach alone is a bad thing; training made up only of negations has to fail. But, oddly enough, many times a negative approach must be taken before the positive aspects of a situation can be emphasized. There must be a combination of both the negative and the positive, and they must be in the right order.

That is proven by Christian experience. If you examine the Scriptures related to the new life after the new birth, you will find that there is negation, but never negation without a challenge. There is never a negative approach to Christian experience without a positive approach along with it.

For example, the Word of God reminds us that we who have been born again are dead to sins, that we might live unto righteousness (I Peter 2:24). Being "dead to sins" is the negative aspect. "Living unto righteousness" is the positive aspect. A great many folk see only the negative side of a Christian life, and their whole life is made up of a series of "don'ts." They make the Christian life so unattractive that people want to avoid it instead of enjoying it.

The purpose of negation in the Christian life is that we might be free to live positively, and such should be the experience of a child who is trained in your home. All the restrictions about which we have been thinking should not be used to build a fence around him and make him feel as if he were in prison; rather, they should free him for the positive approach to life. And so as you bring restrictions into the life of your child, and thus take a negative approach, you must also present a positive approach.

We have been centering our thoughts around one basic verse of Scripture: Proverbs 22:6:

Train up a child in the way he should go: and when he is old, he will not depart from it.

A rather free translation of that verse, based upon the meaning of the various Hebrew words, would have it say, "Train up a child according to his individual bent, and when he reaches the age of maturity he will follow the training he has received."

These first two words "train up" are a translation of the one Hebrew word *kawnak*. We have been looking at various meanings of that word; we now want to look at a final meaning. We shall be considering the word "initiate," which is another meaning of this word *kawnak*.

If you train up a child in the way he should go, you will be initiating him. You will be introducing him to certain truths and practices. You will be acquainting him with concepts with which he will need to be familiar.

Proverbs 29:15 contains a basic principle concerning the initiation of your children. It reveals an attitude that must be maintained:

The rod and reproof give wisdom: but a child left to himself bringeth his mother to shame.

The first part of this verse has been discussed in a general way. Let us now think particularly about the phrase "a child left to himself bringeth his mother to shame." It is easily understandable that a child left to himself will not be a success; he will be a failure. This word translated "left" is interesting in the original text; the Hebrew word speaks of pushing your child away.

There is a very real illustration of this in Job, chapter 30, not from the standpoint of infancy and childhood, but from the standpoint of old age. Job was a man who endured a great deal of suffering. One of the things which he suffered was the indignity of being discriminated against in his old age because of his unattractiveness, the result of suffering and sickness. Verse 12 describes one of these indignities:

Upon my right hand rise the youth; they push away my

feet, and they raise up against me the ways of their destruction.

This situation sometimes presents itself today. Job is saying, "The young men are trying to take away my job. They are trying to pull the rug out from under me. They are pushing me away."

The interesting and important thing is that the words "they push away" in verse 12 are a translation of the same Hebrew word that is translated "left" in Proverbs 29:15.

When we speak of a child's being left to himself, what are we talking about? We are talking about a child who is pushed away. Let us be very practical and very honest. How many times have your children come to you with a question, and you have pushed them away? You were too busy to answer them at that moment. You were engaged in something that you thought was exceedingly important, so you pushed them away—sometimes even physically.

Make a practice of that in your life and your child will eventually get the idea that you do not want to be bothered with his questions. He will also get the idea that if you are not going to give him the information, he will have to work it out for himself. He is then literally "left to himself." Or even more seriously, he may decide that he has to get the information from someone else, and the information he gets that way is not always as accurate as it might be.

How often have you been faced with that question "Why?" At first there is no problem; you give the answer. Then the word comes again, "Why?" By the time it has come three or four times, you probably become impatient and you begin leaving your child to himself. You push him away.

If there is ever a time when your child comes to you with a question, and you have a legitimate reason for not stopping right then and answering the question (there is that possibility; your child may come to you with his question while you are in the midst of a long distance telephone call, for example, and it would be rather foolish to have the person on the other end of the line wait while you go into detail with your child about his question), still, you ought never to push him away. It does not take much time to pause and say something like, "Son, Dad's talking on the telephone right now to a man a long, long way off. As soon as I am through, I will answer your question.''

Genesis 48 contains another suggestion about the attitude that should be maintained as you attempt to initiate your child to various things. In this chapter is found the story of Jacob's blessing the children of Joseph. Keep in mind that Old Testament heads of families had the prophetic power of blessing. I might bless you and you would not be any better off than you were before I blessed you, but individuals in the Old Testament who were the heads of families had a prophetic gift, and whenever they pronounced a blessing on somebody, that blessing came true. In verse 14 we read:

> And Israel stretched out his right hand, and laid it upon Ephraim's head, who was the younger, and his left hand upon Manasseh's head, guiding his hands wittingly; for Manasseh was the firstborn.

We will not go into the details of this passage of Scripture, but basically it says that Jacob put a hand on the head of one boy and the other hand on the head of the other boy.

If a parent never stretches out his hand, literally, to pat his child on the head, the child will bring his mother to shame. We have said a great deal about stretching out your hand and applying it to the place that God made for corporal punishment. But the other end of the subject is of equal importance. Stretch out your hand and pat him on the head, commend him and let him know that you are pleased with what he has done. This is an excellent way of letting him know that you think he is capable of a great deal more than what he has done up to this point.

A child who never receives a pat of commendation, a pat of blessing in this sense, will bring his mother to shame; that is what this passage of Scripture is saying. We need to stop and think about it, because some of us are probably very rigorous about the application of the rod, seeing to it that corporal punishment is carried out. The reason is that the need for corporal punishment is brought so forcefully to our attention. We do not punish our children when they do not deserve it. They have done something and it has been brought to our attention. It is climactic in its effect upon us.

How many times do our children go along doing good and we

never think to stretch out our hand and pat them on the head and say, "We are so proud of you. We appreciate you so much"? In one of the letters I received from my oldest daughter when she was in college, she was asking my advice about doing a certain thing. She listed all the reasons why she wanted to do it. She closed the letter by saying, "But Daddy, I love you. I want to do what you want me to do."

I sat down that same day and wrote to her, which is an unusual thing for me, because I do not write letters very well, nor do I write them very often. But I sat down and wrote to her, and I said, "Honey, the biggest thing about your letter to me is that you said that you want to do what I want you to do. I appreciate that. I love you for it." It was a big thing. I could very easily have neglected to write that letter and have forgotten about it, and she would never have known that one of the most treasured things she said was that she wanted to please me.

We need to take time to stretch out our hand and pat our children on the head, figuratively speaking, because a child that does not receive commendation will bring his parents to shame.

Just as this verse carries the idea of pushing a child away and of neglecting to praise him, it also carries the meaning of "giving up" a child. A child who is given up by his parents brings them to shame.

By that we do not mean a child who is given up for adoption. No matter how old your child may be at this time, if you have not reached the place where you are tempted to give up, you will. You did not think a certain method of training that you had started was going to be very difficult, but you find that it is, and now you are tempted to give up. You find yourself saying, "I have explained it, I have pointed out all the good things about it, and if he does not want to do it, I am through." Have you ever been tempted to say that? Well, you will be. But do not allow yourself to give in to that temptation. Remember that as a parent you do not need to be flattered by the success of your training. You do not give up or hold on simply on the basis of how successful your training is. It is your responsibility as a parent never to give up, never to give in.

There are a great number of parents who did remarkably well for years in the training of their children, but when their children reached a difficult age, they did not follow through with the training. Those children brought their parents to shame.

If we are not to leave our children to themselves to bring their parents to shame, we must come back to the last meaning of our word *kawnak,* which is translated "train up a child" in our key verse, Proverbs 22:6. We must come back to that last meaning, which is "initiate" or "introduce." If your child is to be properly trained, you will have to initiate him to certain facts of life of which he may not be aware, or of which he may have misconceptions unless you initiate him.

Some of the questions that come to mind are: "How do you initiate him? And in relation to what things do you initiate him? How soon do you begin to initiate him along these lines?"

Those questions would be difficult to answer in their entirety, but there is a familiar Old Testament passage of Scripture that offers several guidelines. The Ten Commandments offer a rule of life for initiating your child that will bring about the kind of obedience we would all like to see in the lives of our children.

We will not discuss all of the Commandments, and our purpose here is not to teach their basic meaning; we want to use them only for illustration. You are familiar with the first commandment, as recorded in Exodus 20:3-6:

> 3 Thou shalt have no other gods before me.
> 4 Thou shalt not make unto thee any graven image, or any likeness of anything that is in heaven above, or that is in the earth beneath, or that is in the water under the earth.
> 5 Thou shalt not bow down thyself to them, nor serve them: for I the Lord thy God am a jealous God, visiting the iniquity of the fathers upon the children unto the third and fourth generation of them that hate me;
> 6 And shewing mercy unto thousands of them that love me, and keep my commandments.

You may not have any trouble with your child's making an idol and bowing down and worshiping it, but you will have to initiate him to the fact that God comes first. "Oh," you say, "I think everybody is born with a consciousness of that." No, they are not. Not since the fall of man. In Romans 1:18-21, we have proof of this fact. We find there also an illustration or two of initiating a child to the fact that God comes first:

18 For the wrath of God is revealed from heaven against all ungodliness and unrighteousness of men, who hold the truth in unrighteousness;

19 Because that which may be known of God is manifest in them; for God hath shewed it unto them.

20 For the invisible things of him from the creation of the world are clearly seen, being understood by the things that are made, even his eternal power and Godhead; so that they are without excuse:

21 Because that, when they knew God, they glorified him not as God, neither were thankful; but became vain in their imaginations, and their foolish heart was darkened.

Here is a definite statement that people lost their consciousness of God. If you are to train your child properly, you had better not wait until he is in the junior department of Sunday school before you teach him about God. You had better make him conscious of God from the very first moment you can.

Two things are suggested in this chapter that should help you know when the time for such training has arrived. How did the race originally have the knowledge of God? According to verse 20, they were able to look at the creation and to realize that there was a power behind the creation which they could not see with their naked eyes.

You can get the attention of your child at a very early age. I would not suggest a certain age because I might be making a mistake, and you might think that you do not have to worry about this until your child is that age. Children differ; that is why we have spent so much time on the idea of knowing your individual child. It is enough to say that at a very early age you can take your child outside, point out to him the wonders of nature, and let him know that the wonders of nature are proof that there is a God.

At a very early age, before your child can even talk, you can make him conscious of God by putting his hands together at meal time and teaching him to bow his head while you say a very brief—and this should be emphasized—a very brief prayer of thanksgiving. May I digress, although it is not absolutely a digression, and say that many young people have been turned away from the Lord by unthinking parents who pray long prayers of thanksgiving while the steak and potatoes get cold on the table. The first chance they get, they will rebel at that. It is foolish for your wife to prepare a big meal and then for you to pray while the meal gets cold. You do not have to take that long to thank God for it.

You can teach your child at a very early age to be thankful. He may not even be able to pronounce the word "God," but you are instilling in him the realization that there is a God. If you read these verses in the Book of Romans carefully, you will notice that the reason people forgot about God was that they ceased to be thankful.

In James 1:17 we are told:

> Every good gift and every perfect gift is from above, and cometh down from the Father of lights, with whom is no variableness, neither shadow of turning.

Every time something good happens in your family, you can take the time to tell your children that God is responsible for it. Long before they have any idea of who God is and long before they are able to understand their relationship to Him, they will be conscious of Him.

Why is this so very important? Because if you teach your child that you want him to obey you just because you are you, he will get tired of it some day. But if you teach your child that you want him to obey you because God, who is greater than you, has placed responsibility for him upon your shoulders, he will recognize that disobedience is not only disobedience to you but it is also disobedience to God. That is a deeper thing by far.

Through the years when my children have said, "Daddy, why is it that you keep telling us to do this?" I have said, "Because God put me here a few years before He put you here so that I would be able to guide you across this rough place." It is then not a matter of what I think; it is a matter of what God wants.

Perhaps the significance of this will be more obvious if you will think about another of the Commandments, this one found in verse 12 of Exodus 20:

> Honour thy father and thy mother: that thy days may be long upon the land which the Lord thy God giveth thee.

One of the basic things that you need to teach your child is to honor you, to treat you with esteem, to place a high value on you, and to respect you.

There is in many homes today a distressing habit that parents have allowed their children to fall into, and which serves as an illustration in the matter of honoring parents. It is the custom of children's calling their parents by their first names. It was not intended that you should be a buddy to your child; you were intended to be a parent to your child, and that child ought not to call you by your first name. You ought not to permit it.

You ought to emphasize that you are Father or Mother, or Mama or Daddy, or something else that indicates to your child that you are above him in responsibility and that he must honor you. We have followed a practice in our home of never letting our children be disrespectful to us even in jest. I do not know how many times I have heard little children say "Oh, shut up!" to their parents. They did not really mean it; they were not being ugly; they had just heard that phrase and wanted to express it. I have heard the parents say, "Now, isn't that cute?"

Well, it may be cute right at the moment, but when your child gets to the age of sixteen or so and tells you to shut up, it won't be very cute. We have never permitted our children to say things like that, even in jest. When they were jesting and we knew they were jesting, we always stopped and said, "Now, Daddy knows you are joking, but children must not ever talk to their Daddy or Mother that way. Do not ever do that again."

If they ever did it again we stopped—and I am emphasizing stopping—we stopped and said, "Let me remind you of what we said about that; I am going to have to punish you." We have never followed the practice of saying, "If you ever do that again, I will have to punish you." They understood, and they needed to be reminded by something more forceful than words.

If you put into your child a feeling of respect and honor for you at a very early age, you will not have to instill it in him when he gets older and you are embarrassed by the way he talks to you. Haven't you heard parents say, "I was so embarrassed at the way my son talked to me when you were in my home. I do not know what makes him do that; I am just terribly embarrassed about it"? Well, about all you can do when they are at that age is to be embarrassed. It is too late to do anything about it. Start at the very beginning, because the Bible very definitely says in Romans 1:30 that it is the nature of a child to be disobedient to parents. This is a good illustration of the need of initiation in regard to the relationship that should exist between child and parent.

If you are one of those individuals who say, ''I do not know what has got into him; he is so disobedient,'' you do not know your Bible. It would be much more accurate for you to be surprised when he is obedient. It is a child's nature to be disobedient. The Bible also tells us in II Timothy 3:2 that as we approach the end of the age, one of the indications will be disobedience to parents.

Often we hear arguments that children are no worse today than they were forty years ago—that we just have better means of communication, and thus hear about it a little bit more. That is not true. The Bible emphasizes that toward the end of the age children will be more disobedient. Probably one of the reasons they are more disobedient is that associations are so close now, where once they were not. The standards of parents vary, and children have a lot of support to give them courage to be disobedient.

Why should you teach your child to obey? Why should you initiate him to this truth? Ephesians 6 contains some very practical reasons:

> 1 Children, obey your parents in the Lord: for this is right.
> 2 Honour thy father and mother; which is the first commandment with promise;
> 3 That it may be well with thee, and thou mayest live long on the earth.

You are anxious to do well by your child, aren't you? This is why some of you work as hard as you do. You want to provide things for your child. You want to give him the best, and that is commendable. Now think about this: You are not doing right by your child if you do not teach him to honor you.

Notice that the Bible says this is the only commandment with promise. God has given a special incentive for you to teach your child obedience, and for the child to be obedient. Notice what is said: The child who is obedient will prosper—''that it may be well with thee.''

Most authorities on the subject feel that juvenile delinquency is largely parental delinquency. If the parents are on the ball, generally speaking, juvenile delinquency is not a problem. If you teach your child to obey you and if you teach him to honor you in that obedience, then you are making it possible for him to live well. The child who does not honor you will have a real tendency not to honor God, nor to honor any kind of authority. If you let him get by you, he will find ways to get by every other form of authority. So, just logically thinking, it will not be well with him. But remember also that God has promised long life to the individual who honors his parents.

There are times when God interrupts the normal course of living for purposes known to Himself. There are times when God takes an individual out of this earth, not because he has dishonored his parents, but because He has a special reason for doing so. But all in all, children who honor their parents will live long.

Psychiatrists and social workers tell us that there is a basic relationship between mental and emotional illnesses and physical problems. A child who has been taught to honor his parents will live a calm, normal, natural life, and that in itself will add years to his life span. The emotional stress and strain that many children go through today because they have not been taught this truth quite naturally cuts down on the longevity they ordinarily would have.

There was one statement in this verse that we passed over. We did it purposely so we could think of it last: "Children, obey your parents in the Lord: for this is right." In answer to some of your restrictions, perhaps your child says to you, "I do not see why I have to do that; So-and-So does not have to do it." You may not be able to give a logical reason; there are times when you cannot give a logical reason for obeying.

The trend today seems to be toward the idea that if you disagree with a child, you do not understand him. Have your children ever said to you when it was a matter of obedience, "You just do not understand"? You do understand, and you may give them some very logical reasons, but they do not want to hear them; they close their ears. Their defense is, "You just do not understand."

But if you have taught your child a consciousness of God, you can say at that point, "I do not know that I can give you a reason, except that God says it is right for you to obey me. It is right." Then you can add what is emphasized in Colossians 3:20:

Children, obey your parents in all things: for this is well
pleasing unto the Lord.

"Why do I have to do this? Why do you want me to do it?"
"Because it pleases the Lord for you to do it; that is why."

Incidentally, it would be a good idea for you to become familiar
with these verses of Scripture, because your children eventually
may come to you and say, "All right, where in the Bible does it say
that?" It will not do any good for you to say, "Well, it says it
somewhere; I know it does." If you are not interested enough to
know where it is, you will have great difficulty convincing them
that it is very important.

After making your child conscious of God, there is a further step
that is of great importance. Make your child conscious of God at a
very early age; then as soon as you notice in him any response at all
to spiritual things—any comprehension at all of spiritual truth
—you initiate him, you introduce him, and you acquaint him with
the Lord Jesus Christ. If he does not receive the Lord Jesus Christ,
he cannot be any more concerned about what pleases the Lord and
what does not please the Lord than is any other person who has
never made a profession of faith in Christ.

If an individual has had an experience of grace within his heart,
he is interested in what pleases the Lord. You will find that often
when no other reason will suffice, it will suffice for your children if
you will say to them, "I cannot give you any reason for saying that
you must listen to me in this matter, except that it will please the
Lord." Many times they will follow your instructions just for that
reason when they would for no other.

Consider the rest of the Commandments. You need to initiate
your child, for example, to the fact that he should not lie. Do not
wait until he has formed a habit of lying and then try to break the
habit. Let him know from the very beginning that truth is better
than lies. "Oh," you say, "Maybe he never will learn how to lie."
The Bible does not say that. The Bible says in Psalm 58:3 that your
child, that every child, goes astray from the womb, speaking lies as
soon as he is born. Your child will begin to deceive you long before
you think he knows enough to deceive you. You will have to be
pretty alert. If you become exasperated at that, just remember that

he has learned a great deal from you and your actions.

The Bible says in Psalm 119 that God hates every false way. Did you notice what it says? *Every* false way. There are any number of parents who are concerned about their children's lying when their children see them deceive almost every day of their lives. It is very hard for a child to understand why he should not lie when he knows that his parents do.

For example, you may tell your child that you will do something for him, and then you get busy doing something else. He comes along at the appointed time and reminds you that you agreed to do that thing for him, but you are busy now on something else. You say, "Run along now; I do not have time." He says, "But, Daddy, you promised." What you do not realize is that when he says, "Daddy, you promised," he is giving you an opportunity not to be a liar, but you do not take advantage of it. He may never tell you, but in his own little heart he says, "My Daddy is a liar. He said he would do something, and he did not do it."

How many times have you told your children, "I do not want you to do so-and-so." Then you get busy about something; they do the forbidden thing, and you do not fulfill your word about the restriction. They gradually realize that you are a liar—that you do not mean what you say.

How many times have they heard your telephone conversation and known from the very conversation that you were a liar? Oh, it is a little white lie; nothing too big. How many times have you been talking with someone on the telephone and you are tired of talking, and you say, "I think there is somebody at the door"? Then you hang up the phone, and you know and your child knows that there is nobody at the door. Of course you did not say there was somebody at the door; you only said you thought there was. You see, they know you lie, and they cannot see why it is so important for them not to lie when you lie with such freedom. You need to initiate them to truth, and not just reproach them for lying.

There is one other suggestion that can be gleaned from the Commandments. It concerns the time of initiating children. How soon, for example, would you try to initiate them to a consciousness of God? You cannot begin too soon. Long before we had any children, a very lovely woman who was much concerned about training her children for the Lord told my wife and me something that we have never forgotten. She said that as she leaned over the crib of her babies, even right after they were born, she sang little gospel choruses that had in them the names of Jesus and God. She felt that their little minds could gradually get the idea, young as they were. She said she even repeated a verse of Scripture as she tucked them in bed at night.

Maybe no one will ever be able to prove how much a little infant can absorb from a crooning lullaby with a Christian message from the lips of its mother, but you certainly cannot do any harm in that way. You could do a great deal of good.

So how soon do we begin with some of these things? At a very early age. But how soon with other things? Know your child; be alert. For example, there is a commandment about adultery. That would be a rather foolish thing about which to talk with your four-year-old child.

My wife tells a story along this line that has always amused me. She says that when she was about five years of age, she was sitting in a room with adults and they were talking about some folks who had committed adultery. It was a new word; she had never heard it before, so when the visitors left she asked, "Mother, what is adultery?" It flustered Mother to have that asked so pointedly by a young child; she did not quite know how to answer, and what she said was, "Oh, it's something that adults do."

That was pretty apt, and it did satisfy the child's curiosity at the moment. You certainly do not want to talk about the commandment against adultery to a four-year-old child, but you do not want your young son to learn about adultery in a manner that would cause problems, either. You had better know him, and when your boy is old enough to begin to ask questions, do not shut him off. Do not say, "Don't talk about things like that." Answer whatever question about sex that you can, practically and legitimately.

Your daughter needs to know, too. Incidentally, there is something wrong with your approach to sex if you as a father cannot talk to your daughter about sex. If she has the idea that the only one who can discuss the subject with her is her mother, because they both are females, then somehow you have left the wrong impression. Fathers ought to be able to talk as freely with their daughters about sex as their mothers can. And by the same token, mothers ought to be able to talk as freely with their sons as their fathers can.

We have emphasized consistently that it is the responsibility of the father to undergird the weight of training the child. It is no different when it comes to the matter of sex.

When my oldest son was twelve years of age, he and I went on a trip together. I have always prayed that the Lord would make me alert to the needs of my children, and I knew from something he had said that we needed to talk about this subject. I let him lead. I did not plan to tell him any more than he needed to know, but I found out that he needed to know a great deal. After our conversation I said to him, "These things that we have talked about are not things to be laughed about; they are not things to make jokes about. They are not things to say in a way that makes people giggle. I have told you everything there is to be told. If there is something that is not clear to you, when you want to know about it you can come and ask me. But I am going to be terribly disappointed in you if you stand around with the boys, joking and talking about things related to sex in an unlovely way. Remember, there is not one thing that they can tell you that I have not already told you. I know and they do not. They are just kids. If that sort of thing ever comes up, the thing for you to do is say, 'Fellows, I know all about that; my Dad told me,' and just walk away."

Sex is a most sacred thing when it is rightly related to God. I think many of our children and our young people are terribly confused, simply because the subject has not been approached in a clean, clear way.

My oldest daughter came home one day when she was in elementary school, very much disturbed about some things that happened related to sex. She talked to her mother first, and then her mother said, "Why don't you go talk to Daddy?" She came into my study and said, "Daddy, I have to talk to you about this." She was tremendously upset by the thing that had happened. I took her on my lap there in my study, and I answered honestly every question that she asked. She has a healthy approach toward sex today.

This subject is nothing to be ashamed of. The facts of life are something to which you should initiate your child. If you do, you will save yourself a lot of grief and a great many problems. Remember this: His questions are going to be answered, and if you do not answer them, somebody else will.

When to answer them? In regard to a knowledge of God, you cannot begin too soon. In regard to other matters such as sex, whenever the real need appears.

Do not think that all children will be the same. When my younger son was thirteen years of age I had not told him half of what I had told his older brother at the age of twelve, because his questions were different. They came in installments. He would ask one question and get the answer. He would examine that every way, and if he could accept it, that was all he would want to know at that particular time. Later he would come with another question. We would discuss it in detail and he would be satisfied. His introduction to these matters was just as thorough, but handled in a quite different way from that of his brother. Let the Holy Spirit guide you. Study your child. Know your individual child. As you learn to know him, you will know what to say and what to do.

10

Your Well-Disciplined Child Is Your Recommendation

We want to leave with you some Scripture passages that may not present anything new but which, hopefully, will summarize the matters we have discussed. These are passages at which for the most part we have not looked, or which we may have mentioned only in passing. With these Scriptures, we shall try to tie up all the loose ends by way of summary.

The first Scripture reference is found in Paul's first letter to Timothy, chapter 5. Here we find emphasized again the responsibility of parents in bringing children into the world. If we fail to keep that responsibility in mind, then all of these things that we have been saying about child training are unimportant. If, on the other hand, there is a real recognition of responsibility for the bearing of children, the responsibility of training them will be recognized much more clearly.

There are a number of exhortations concerning widows, both young and older women, in this chapter. In the day in which these words were written, it was the responsibility of the church to look after widows. In most cases, there was no other means of support for them. Verses 9 through 13 of the chapter give some requirements that the widows had to meet. This passage of Scripture is a cause for concern to some. It does not mean that if a woman could not meet these requirements she could not be a member of the church. It does mean, however, that she would not be eligible for financial or material help. The church would not look after widows who did not meet these requirements. Verses 11, 12, and 13 contain a specific reference to young widows. The church is not to support them, the Scripture says, because that would give them a lot of free time to wander about and do nothing but gossip. It would give them time to associate with unbelievers, and to marry unbelievers and cast off their first faith. The passage does not suggest that there is anything wrong with a young widow's marrying again, but it does teach that it is wrong to use time unwisely.

Verse 14 is the one in which we are interested:

> I will therefore that the younger women marry, bear children, guide the house, give none occasion to the adversary to speak reproachfully.

Here it is emphasized again that young women should accept the God-given responsibility of bringing children into the world. A young woman's responsibility is to marry, to bear children, to guide the house, and to give none occasion to the adversary to speak reproachfully.

These verses emphasize that this is the primary responsibility of the young woman. Of course, there are exceptions; it is not God's will for all women to marry. By the same token, there are some married women from whom God withholds children for reasons known only to Himself. These women should in no way be criticized. But the general standard is that God expects women to do these things, and it is only when they make an effort to do so that they will be able to "give none occasion to the adversary to speak reproachfully."

The last part of this statement is a very good thing to keep in mind. Through the years I have dealt with many marital problems that have arisen because young women, without realizing what they are doing, were giving occasion to the adversary by refusing to stay at home and to guide the house. Because they were out in the world keeping company that was not advisable, their marriages were broken up. So we emphasize that the responsibility of child bearing is not one that can be rejected or refused.

In chapter 12 of II Corinthians Paul emphasizes a truth along this same line. It is a basic fact, and it needs to be kept in mind. We have emphasized that your children should come first with you. Your first thought, your first interest, should be for them and for their welfare. Many people today suggest, however, that your children ought not to fill your time; you have an obligation to do this thing or that thing; your children need not be the center of your attention. Notice in verse 14 what Paul had to say:

Behold, the third time I am ready to come to you; and I will not be burdensome to you; for I seek not yours, but you: for the children ought not to lay up for the parents, but the parents for the children.

The last part of that verse is the statement of a principle, and Paul uses it to illustrate his concern for these Corinthian believers. He looked upon these believers of Corinth as his children in the faith, and to them he said, ''I do not want to be burdensome to you; I am not seeking what you have. I am seeking to help you, and I am following a principle when I do that. That principle is this: Children ought not to have to provide for the parents, but the parents ought to provide for the children.''

The principle advocated in many quarters today that children owe their parents something is contrary to Scripture. The Scripture does say that children owe their parents respect, and other passages of Scripture, such as I Timothy 5:8, say that if children do not requite their parents they are worse than infidels. But the principle of Scripture is that as far as provision goes, your whole life as a parent should be geared around your children. You ought to be laying up financially for them, whenever that is possible. You ought to be laying aside resources with their future needs and interests at heart, if that is at all possible.

This principle might have some effect on the decisions you will make. For example, you might be living on a certain economic level, and you see the possibility of moving up to another level. But to do that you might in the future have to deny your children some very important provisions. Your children should come first. Based on this principle, such a move should not be made. You should lay up for your children and not ask, or force, them to deny themselves for you.

So recognize that there is a responsibility for child bearing, and recognize that you have a responsibility to put your children first, above every other consideration.

Notice how the Holy Spirit describes the growth of the Lord

Jesus Christ from childhood through adolescence to maturity. It should emphasize to our hearts the kind of growth we should expect in our own children, and the emphasis that should be placed accordingly. We recognize that Jesus Christ is the Son of God, and because He is, we might be inclined to think that His earthly parents had nothing at all to do with His training and His preparation for the task for which He came to the earth. But if you examine what the Bible has to say about His childhood, adolescence, and growth to maturity, you will find that this is not the case.

It is interesting that the writer who directs our attention to this more than the other Gospel writers is Luke, the physician. He recognized its importance just as a family doctor today recognizes that many of the ills of children can be traced back to their training or their lack of training. Doctor Luke recognized the importance of the proper and careful training of the Lord Jesus.

In Luke 2 we find the record of the birth of Christ and His presentation at the temple when He was eight days old, His return to His home, the time He spent there until He was twelve years of age, His journey back to Jerusalem, His return again to His home, and His life from the age of twelve to maturity. Two passages stand out in that chapter by way of comparison and contrast. One of them is verse 40:

> And the child grew, and waxed strong in spirit, filled with wisdom: and the grace of God was upon him.

This describes the growth of Jesus from infancy to the age of twelve. Now look at verses 51 and 52:

> 51 And he went down with them, and came to Nazareth, and was subject unto them. . . .
> 52 And Jesus increased in wisdom and stature, and in favour with God and man.

They describe the growth of Jesus from the age of twelve to maturity, to when He entered His public ministry at the age of thirty.

Before we go any further, let us recognize that there were some things about the Lord Jesus Christ that would not be true of every child, because Jesus was the Son of God. Therefore it is not strange to hear Him saying, "How is it that ye sought me? Wist ye not that

I must be about my Father's business?'' That would be a ridiculous thing for an ordinary child to say.

But keep in mind that although the Lord Jesus Christ did not enter public life until the age of thirty, it does not necessarily follow that children of today should wait until that age before they depart from home and enter public life. Situations change. People are more mature at an early age during certain eras than they are during other eras, because of conditions in society. So we will not be sticklers about the specific age of maturity. But we will emphasize the difference between growth and training in childhood, and growth and training in adolescence and toward maturity.

With that thought in mind, look again at verse 40:

> And the child grew, and waxed strong . . . filled with wisdom: and the grace of God was upon him.

We purposely leave out the words "in spirit" because they are not in the original text. You will notice three things in this verse of Scripture: There was development physically, there was development mentally, and there was development spiritually.

If you would examine in the original text the word translated "grew," you would find that it describes a process that is carried on more or less as a normal thing, without a great deal of prodding, or effort on the part of the child. It is just a normal, ordinary thing.

I would suggest about your child that you should watch over these areas of growth . . . guiding, shaping as you might a young plant, but—and this is very important—not forcing. Never force the growth.

This forcing of growth is one of the mistakes made by many parents; they try to make their children older than they actually are. That is one of the causes for concern about our present-day society. For instance, boys who ought to be interested in ordinary pursuits such as football and fishing are being pushed onto the dance floor before they are interested in dancing.

My sons have received invitations to dance clubs as early as age eleven. You know very well that it is not the children of that age who are interested in such clubs; it is the parents who are interested.

That is an illustration of forcing growth. In the life of our Lord before the age of twelve, His was a natural growth, a normal thing.

But you will notice that He grew. This is a reference to His physical growth and development. Then we are told that He waxed strong in spirit, filled with wisdom. That is a reference to His mental growth. Then we are told that the grace of God was upon Him.

Your child should grow mentally. You should observe him, and if he is not progressing in the way that he should, you should be concerned enough to do something about it. Investigate it; see what can be done. You ought to be interested in his mental growth.

Notice what is said about the spiritual growth of the Lord: "The grace of God was upon him. . . ." Lead your child to the Lord, and let the grace of God take over normally in his life. Teach him the Word of God, as has been pointed out, but do not force the issue. Just let the grace of God be upon him.

The Scripture constantly emphasizes that a child, when introduced to the things of God, will normally follow along that line without being forced or being pushed into it. There will be times, to be sure, when the old nature with which he is equipped will make itself evident, but usually when children are young they will have inclinations along spiritual lines. For example, they will want to pray about everything—their puppy, their playmates, their activities of the day—everything.

You should not discourage that, even though it may seem ridiculous. You will find that after they reach a certain age, usually about twelve, and enter into their teens, they are not so anxious to pray about all those things.

That brings us to the second phase of the growth of the Lord. Verse 51 of Luke 2 tells us that He went down to Nazareth and was subject to His mother and father. He never failed to be subject unto them until the day when, as Messiah, He had to sever His earthly family connections. When He said, "Who is my mother, my father, my brethren? Are not all of you?" (Matt. 12:48), He was severing all family connections for a purpose.

During all this period of growth He was subject to His parents. That does not mean that they were telling Him what to do in every instance. He was the One that was doing, but it was all subject to their direction.

I have mentioned this before, but I want to emphasize it again. A thing that my wife and I have consistently prayed about is that the

Lord will let us know when to let our children go—when to let them begin to make the decisions—when to let them begin to go this way or that. Some would say, "Oh, that is simple. When they want to do a certain thing, let them do it." That is not necessarily the wise thing to do. There are many children who want to do things they are not capable of doing. If you wait upon the Lord, He can make you alert so that you just stand in the background, so to speak, watching over the whole thing as they make their decisions.

Notice again verse 52:

> And Jesus increased in wisdom and stature, and in favour with God and man.

The first thing we should notice about this verse is the word "increased." It is a translation of an entirely different Greek word from the word translated "grew" in verse 40. The word "grew" in that verse suggests natural growth and development, but this word "increased" is a translation of the Greek word *enkopto,* and it speaks of cutting down trees, of hewing out a trail, and of active, energetic force.

Here we learn that Jesus in His active early years grew like any other child. But after He began to advance from adolescence into maturity, He took the bull by the horns, so to speak, and began to make conscious progress on His own—always, however, under the supervision of His parents.

There are some parents who never let their children get to that place. They make the decisions for them, and they tell them what to do and how to do it. Then they thrust them out into life where they have to make their own decisions, and the children do not have any idea what to do because they are in the habit of having everything done for them.

Notice, too, a difference in emphasis in this verse. The first thing that is mentioned in the period before the age of twelve is physical growth, and that is important. You ought to be concerned about your child's physical development. But the first thing that is mentioned in verse 52 in describing the adolescent years is mental growth. He increased in wisdom. That is where the emphasis is placed—on wisdom.

The next thing that is mentioned is that He grew in stature, which is a recognition of His physical growth. The third thing that we see is a reference to His spiritual growth. It is very interesting to notice how it is stated: He grew "in favour with God and man. . . ."

That is the way the King James Version translates it. If this were really what it says, it would indicate to us that the longer He lived, the more kindly other men thought of Him, but that is not what the text really says. What it does say is that He "grew in favour," and the word "favour" is a translation of the Greek word for "grace"; He grew in grace beside God and beside men.

We all know individuals who are well versed in the Scripture and are well versed in spiritual things, but who are complete misfits in their relationship to society. They do not seem to have a proper balance. In many instances, this is because their parents did not train them with that balance in mind.

All that is said about the grace of God in the life of Jesus before the age of twelve is that "the grace of God was upon him." That is all. But after the age of twelve He began to grow in the grace and the knowledge of God. This leads me to suggest that you should not be too discouraged if you do not see in your children in their early years all the growth in spiritual maturity that you would like to see.

They may not be as deeply versed in spiritual things as you would like for them to be. But after they reach a certain age, if it is twelve—here again it should be emphasized that it may be a different age for each child—if there is not any real growth after that, you need to be concerned. If they are still praying little "Now I lay me down to sleep" prayers at the age of fourteen, you need to be concerned. They are not growing spiritually.

It is all right for them to pray about a lot of little things that seem ridiculous to you when they are little, but if they are still praying that way in their teenage years, it is an indication that they have not grown, and you need to be concerned about it.

If we are to train our children, let us be sure that their training is in all three of these fields in the early years—just letting them grow, so to speak, with gentle tending. After that time, recognize that the growth is going to be faster, and more diligence and effort on the part of the parents will be needed to direct the growth.

Another strong emphasis that we have tried to make in this study is the absolute need for discipline. For example, we looked at

Proverbs 29:15, where we learned that a child left to himself will bring his mother to shame. Discipline is necessary. Almost anyone will agree to that. But the problem here lies in extremes of discipline.

There are two passages of Scripture which emphasize the two extremes that make discipline a problem. The first one is Proverbs 22:15. We have mentioned this passage before, but we refer to it again for emphasis. This verse reveals the problem with which some people are faced when they fear that their discipline may be excessive:

> Foolishness is bound in the heart of a child; but the rod of correction shall drive it far from him.

In the next chapter, verse 13, is a passage that is truly applicable to a great many families:

> Withhold not correction from the child: for if thou beatest him with the rod, he shall not die.

The Holy Spirit has used extreme language here for the sake of emphasis. He is not suggesting that you use corporal punishment to the extent of physical injury. What He is saying is something like this: "You never punish your child physically; you act as if you are afraid you will kill him if you do. Well, do not worry; you won't kill him. He will live through it."

The extreme that some people face is that of withholding corporal punishment entirely because they cannot bear to inflict injury of any kind. The old adage that we perhaps have used, "This hurts me more than it does you," has a lot of truth to it. Most of us refrain from corporal punishment because we hate to think about hurting the child that we love, and if we go ahead with the punishment, it really does hurt us more than it does the child.

There is a certain sense in which restraint is needed, but there is also a need for emphasis upon not being too fearful in the correction of your child. Do not be too afraid to correct him; he will live through it.

Paul's letter to the Colossians presents the other side of the problem. We need to recognize a happy medium in this training. We can be too hesitant to discipline—there is no question about that—but on the other hand, we can be unreasonable in our discipline. Colossians 3:17-21 says:

> 17 And whatsoever ye do in word or deed, do all in the name of the Lord Jesus, giving thanks to God and the Father by him.
> 18 Wives, submit yourselves unto your own husbands, as it is fit in the Lord.
> 19 Husbands, love your wives, and be not bitter against them.
> 20 Children, obey your parents in all things: for this is well pleasing to the Lord.
> 21 Fathers, provoke not your children to anger, lest they be discouraged.

These verses relate to family relationships. Many people begin reading this paragraph with verse 18 because they think it begins there, but the thought actually begins in verse 17.

The only way you will have a happy relationship in your home—of wife to husband, of husband to wife, of parents to children—is to instill in the hearts of your children the knowledge that everything is being done in the name of the Lord Jesus Christ.

For example, you should not demand obedience from your children simply on the basis that you are their parents. You should instill in them the realization that you are making these requests of them in the name of the Lord Jesus Christ. You should instill in them the idea that what you are doing is not a personal thing, but you are doing it as a representative of the Lord Jesus Christ. That will make your correction of them easier for them to bear, because the personal aspect will be eliminated.

I recall a two-hour conference with a seventeen-year-old girl who was on the verge of an emotional breakdown. All the time she and her mother were in my presence she was screaming out, "I hate my mother! I hate her!" Those were not just the words of a spoiled brat. She is young woman with a real problem. Somewhere in the process of correction it had become a personal battle between the mother and the daughter. It was not a relationship between Christ, the mother, and the daughter.

Verse 21 of Colossians 3 also has a very important message:

> Fathers, provoke not your children to anger, lest they be discouraged.

It is possible for you as a parent to be so hesitant to administer discipline that you do your child an injustice. On the other hand, you can be so particular about every slight infraction that you provoke your children to anger. For example, you have probably heard of children who turn on their parents, stamp their feet and say, "I hate you!" as did the girl I mentioned. Sometimes that is the result of poor training, but at other times it is because the parents have provoked the child to that kind of action.

Then notice the last part of that statement: "lest they be discouraged." The suggestion here is that you can be so strict with your child that you can discourage him. He may reach the point where he says, "What's the use? Nothing I do pleases you. Nothing is ever right, so what's the use of trying?" He is discouraged to the point of disobedience.

Notice that these words are addressed to the father. It is not the mother who provokes the child as a rule. The mother has the responsibility of routine discipline, and she usually has time to think about the discipline she administers. But the father usually deals with the big things, and these things are often presented to him on the spur of the moment. He may not take the time to pray about it to seek the direction of the Lord. He flails out with his discipline. He is angry and provoked, and it rubs off on the child. Fathers have a real responsibility.

That leads us back to say that if we as parents carry on our discipline in the name of the Lord Jesus Christ, we will be concerned about the reaction of our children to discipline. I have heard parents say, "I do not care whether he likes it or not. I told him to do it, and he is going to do it." You had better care, because he could very well form from the way you discipline him an opinion of the Lord Jesus Christ that would be dishonoring to Christ, and that might even turn him against Christ.

Ephesians 6:4 is almost a repetition of these words. But in this instance a substitute for provocation is suggested:

> And, ye fathers, provoke not your children to wrath: but bring them up in the nurture and admonition of the Lord.

Do not provoke them to wrath, but rather bring them up in the admonition of the Lord, the understanding of the Lord, letting them know that your correction of them is related to God's will for their lives and to His will for your lives as a family.

An impressive thought, and one that many, many folk do not

understand, is that your correction of your children will determine your usefulness to God. Think about that! Your correction of your children is one of the factors in determining your usefulness to God. When you have the time to do so carefully, read chapter 18 of the Book of Genesis. There you will read how God was willing to trust Abraham with a very real secret, because He said, "I know [Abraham], and I know that he will command his children . . . after me" (Gen. 18:19). The idea was that if you could trust him to guide his children rightly, you could trust him to administer the things of God rightly. This same thought is emphasized in the New Testament in I Timothy 3. Here are presented the requirements for the leadership of the church today—the requirements for bishops and the requirements for deacons.

We have many types of leadership in our churches today—youth workers, Sunday school teachers, and others—that they did not have in the early church. I have always been of the opinion, and I have taught, that regardless of the place of leadership in the church today, the requirements for those in leadership ought to be the same as the requirements for the leadership of the church in the days when organization was very simple. Notice what I Timothy 3:2-5 has to say:

> 2 A bishop then must be blameless, the husband of one wife, vigilant, sober, of good behaviour, given to hospitality, apt to teach;
> 3 Not given to wine, no striker, not greedy of filthy lucre; but patient, not a brawler, not covetous;
> 4 One that ruleth well his own house, having his children in subjection with all gravity;
> 5 (For if a man know not how to rule his own house, how shall he take care of the church of God?).

There are not many people who realize that the way you train your children fits you for service in the church, but that is what God says in His Word. If you do not know how to train your own children, then you should not be trying to take spiritual leadership in the church. God is saying that if you fail with your own family, how could you possibly be trusted with the welfare of the souls of men?

Look at verse 12, where the office of deacon is mentioned:

> Let the deacons be the husband of one wife, ruling their children and their own houses well.

A well-disciplined household is a recommendation for spiritual leadership. Do you see how this is involved in so many things that we do, and cannot be taken lightly? How many times has it been said of certain spiritual leaders, "They are fine men, but oh, their children!" Sometimes such statements are unfair; sometimes the criticism is unjust. Someone may say, "What difference does it make?" God says it makes a great deal of difference. The training of your child is a recommendation of your service for the Lord.

The last passage I want to mention is Psalm 127. Perhaps you are young enough that you have not seen the truth of this psalm in its entirety, but the day will come when you will. I offer this to you as something to which you can look forward, something which will bring real satisfaction:

> 3 Lo, children are an heritage of the Lord: and the fruit of the womb is his reward.

We have emphasized previously that we believe that children are divinely given. This passage of Scripture bears that out:

> 4 As arrows are in the hand of a mighty man; so are children of the youth.
> 5 Happy is the man that hath his quiver full of them: they shall not be ashamed, but they shall speak with the enemies in the gate.

Here the psalmist compares children to arrows. He says, "Happy is the man that has his quiver full." I have said, facetiously sometimes, but more seriously than one might think, that you ought to have your quiver full. You are not doing God justice, and you are not doing yourself justice, unless you do.

Not everybody has the same-sized quiver. One family's quiver may be full with one or two. It took seven to fill mine. It may take twelve to fill yours. I do not know, and it is not for me to say. But it is important to have your quiver full, because children are like arrows in the hand of a mighty man.

What do you do with an arrow? You put it in the bow, you bend the bow, you pull back the bowstring, and you let fly the arrow. My, what a satisfaction it is, what real joy it is, when you see the arrow hit the target. You realize that you have been able to do through your children what you never could have done yourself.

Now wait just a moment. This is not to say that you impose your ambitions on the child. We have dealt with that. This is not to say that because you always wanted to be a missionary, and couldn't, you are going to make sure that one of your children is a missionary. My suggestion is that although you are one and only one, if you have your quiver full of arrows, as you shape and bend the bow you can launch the arrows, and when an arrow hits the mark you will realize for the first time what real satisfaction is.

Perhaps you have had a certain amount of satisfaction in life up to this point because you have attained certain goals. You may not have attained all of your goals, but you have attained some of them, and you have had a certain satisfaction because you did. But whatever satisfaction you may have had in attaining goals for yourself is nothing compared with the satisfaction you will have when you see your arrows hit the mark that you have trained them to hit. Then every sleepless night, every financial sacrifice, every physical sacrifice that you have ever made, will seem worthwhile. But remember this: The arrows will never hit the mark that they should unless they are launched in the right direction. That is where your responsibility and mine lies.

7J